The All-Seeing Unseen Eye of God, and Other Sermons
By Matthew Newcomen

The All-Seeing Unseen Eye of God, and Other Sermons
By Matthew Newcomen

Edited and updated by C. Matthew McMahon and Therese B. McMahon
Transcribed by Blake Gentry

Published by Puritan Publications
A Ministry of A Puritan's Mind
4101 Coral Tree Circle #214
Coconut Creek, FL 33073
www.puritanshop.com
www.apuritansmind.com
www.puritanpublications.com

This Print Edition, 2013
Electronic Edition, 2013
Manufactured in the United States of America

ISBN: 978-1-62663-049-9
eISBN: 978-1-62663-048-2

TABLE OF CONTENTS

MEET MATTHEW NEWCOMEN

Matthew Newcomen (1610–1669), ejected minister, and one of the authors of "SMECTYMNUS", born at Colchester about 1610, was second son of Stephen Newcomen by his first wife, and second cousin of Elias Newcomen. The father was the third son of John Newcomen, and Alice, daughter of John Gascoigne of Leasingcroft, Yorkshire. He was grandson of Brian, and great-grandson of Martyn le Newcomen (d. 1536), all of Saltfleetby, Lincolnshire. He was presented to the vicarage of St. Peter's, Colchester, on July 18, 1600, and was enrolled a burgess of the town (Morant MSS. Colchester Museum). His will was proved on May 31, 1631.

Matthew was educated under William Kempe at the Royal Grammar School of Colchester, and on Nov. 8, 1626 was elected the second scholar on the foundation of "Robert Lewis and Mary his wife," at St. John's College, Cambridge. He graduated with a B.A. in 1629, and an M.A. in 1633. Dr. Edmund Calamy says, "he was much esteemed as a wit, and for his curious parts, which being afterwards sanctified by Divine grace fitted him for eminent service in the church." On the death of John Rogers on Oct. 18, 1636, Newcomen was recommended by his friend John Knowles (1600?–1685), then lecturer at Colchester, to the lectureship, which was supported by voluntary contributions at Dedham, seven miles off.

Newcomen soon became the leader of the church reform party in Essex. He married the sister of Calamy's wife, and assisted Calamy to write, "Smectymnuus" published in London in 1641. The authors at once became marked men, and on Nov. 24th, when Newcomen preached at the weekly lecture at Stowmarket, where Thomas Young, another Smectymnuan, was vicar, there were an, "abundance of ministers," and a quart of wine was, "sent for" at the lecture dinner (Churchwarden's accounts in Hollingsworth's *Hist. of Stowmarket*, pp. 146, 189).

Newcomen, who drew up a catechism with John Arrowsmith (1602–1659) and Anthony Tuckney, was chosen one of the Westminster divines, and preached the opening sermon before the assembly and both houses of parliament on the afternoon of Saturday, July 7, 1643. He wishes that, "their traducers might be witnesses of their learned, grave, and pious debates." He was on the third committee, which met in the Jerusalem Chamber, and was to deal with Articles 8, 9, and 10. He was also on committees to, "consider a way of expediting the examination of ministers," to

5

inquire of scandalous books, to petition parliament, and to communicate with the Scottish assembly.

Newcomen did not sign the petition for the Presbyterian form of church government presented by the Essex and Suffolk clergy on May 29, 1646, but he drew up and signed, with one hundred and twenty-nine others, the, "Testimony of the Ministers in Essex," London, 1648.

When the, "Agreement" was sent down for the signatures of the clergy, Essex men were again in arms, and headed by Rogers of Wethersfield, Collins of Braintree, Newcomen and his friend, George Smith, vicar of Dedham, they drew up, "The Essex Watchmen's Watchword," London, 1649, protesting against evils lurking under its proposals, and especially against, "one parenthesis [proposing toleration], which like the fly in the box of ointment may make it abhorrent in the nostrils of everyone who is judicious and pious."

Newcomen was appointed an assistant to the commission of, "Triers of Scandalous Ministers," &c., for Essex in 1654. In 1655 he was town lecturer at Ipswich (Browne, *Hist. of Congregationalism in Norfolk and Suffolk*, pp. 152, 157). He refused the office of chaplain to Charles II at the *Restoration*, although Calamy, Young, Manton, Spurstowe, and others accepted. He was a member of the Savoy conference in 1660, "the most constant," Baxter wrote, "in assisting us." On Oct. 10, 1661 he was awarded a D.D. But, "for such a man to declare unfeigned assent and consent, as required by the Act of Uniformity, was impossible," (David's, *Hist. of Evangel. Nonconf. in Essex*). He preached his last sermon as lecturer at Dedham, on

Aug. 20, 1662, on Rev. 3:3. He urged those, "unable to enjoy public helps for sanctifying the Lord's Day at home, to travel to other congregations, or to redouble their fervor in secret and family devotion." A few weeks later he preached, "Ultimum Vale, or the Last Farewell of a Minister of the Gospel to a beloved People," in London, 1663.

On July 30, 1662 the English community at Leyden was authorized by the magistrate to call Newcomen from Dedham. In December following he accepted the call, and became pastor of the English church there. Professor Hornbeck, and many others of the university, appreciated his abilities. In 1668 his congregation voted him a yearly salary of one thousand florins, with an additional five hundred on Feb. 1, 1669 (Leyden *Stadtarchiv*).

The name of, "Newcomen, a minister," was included among fourteen persons warned to return home by a royal proclamation issued March 26, 1666, signed by Charles II on April 9, (*State Papers, Dom.* 1665–6, pp. 318, 342), but it was struck out owing to personal influence. Sir John Webster, under date March 5, 1667, wrote to the king from abroad, begging license to remain for himself, and also for, "Mr. [Matthew] Newcomen, a poore preacher at Leyden, that hath a sicke wife and five poore and sicklye children. He came out of England with license, and liveth peaceably, not meddling with anie affaires in England, hath done nothing towards printing or dispersing bookes, and has constantly prayed for the King and Council. He humbly craveth to be exempt from the summons, and is readye to purge himself by word or oath before any Comissary yr. Majie. may appoint." Webster says he writes at, "the entreaty of several persons of respect, and by Mr. Richard Maden, preacher at Amsterdam" (ib. 1666-7, p. 549).

Newcomen died at Leyden about Sept. 1, 1669 of the plague. On Sept. 16th his funeral sermon was preached at Dedham by John Fairfax (1623-1700), ejected minister of Barking, Suffolk. Great numbers were present, and in the returns made to Sheldon that year the service is spoken of as, "an outrageous conventicle." The sermon was published under the title of, "The Dead Saint yet Speaking," London, 1679. Newcomen's widow was granted on March 13, 1670 permission to sell his books, and on April 8th she, meaning to return to England, was voted five hundred florins, "in consideration of the good services of her deceased husband, and of her receiving as guests the preachers who came to Leyden since his death about seven months ago" (Leyden *Stadtarchiv*). Newcomen's house at Dedham, "which cost him 600£," was purchased from his representatives in 1703 by a successor in the lectureship, William Burkitt the commentator, and, together with a sum collected by him, settled upon the lecturers (*Letter from Burkitt*, quoted in *The Church in Dedham in the Seventeenth Century* by the Rev. G. Taylor, D.C.L., lecturer, 1868).

Newcomen married in 1640 Hannah, daughter of Robert Snelling, M.P. for Ipswich 1614-25, sister of Edmund Calamy's first wife, and widow of Gilbert Reyney or Rany, rector of St. Mary's Stoke, Ipswich. Newcomen was her third husband, the first being one Prettiman (Hunter MSS.) Four sons and seven daughters were born to Newcomen at Dedham, but six died in early childhood, and were buried there. There were living in 1667 Stephen, baptized on

Sept. 17, 1645; Hannah, baptized on March 9, 1647; Martha, March 30, 1651; Alice, July 25, 1652; and Sarah, Aug. 26, 1655. Stephen was inscribed a member of Leyden University on May 28, 1663, as a, "student in philosophy." It is probable that he was the father of Stephen Newcomen, vicar of Braintree 1709–38, donor to that living of a considerable sum of money as well as curious communion plate, and vicar of Boreham, Essex, from 1738 until his death, July 15, 1750, aged 72.

Matthew Newcomen is said to have written a work called, "Irenicum," which must not be confounded with Stillingfleet's, "Irenicum, a Weapon Salve for the Church's Wounds," 1662. He also published seven sermons separately, and is stated by Hunter (Chorus Vatum) to have written verses on the death of Richard Vines.

For further study see:

Calamy and Palmer's *Nonconf. Memorial*, ii. 195–8, Continuation, ii. 294, Abridgement, p. 212; Neal's *Hist. of Puritans*, iv. 389, 390 n.; Baxter's *Reliquiæ* pp. 229, 232, 281, 303–7; Mitchell's *Westminster Assembly*, pp. xviii, 138, 296, and his *Minutes of the Session*, pp. 304, 409, 419, 420, 423; Kennett's Register, pp. 162, 188, 295, 398, 431, 546, 900; Stevens' *Hist. of the Scottish Church in Rotterdam*, p. 315; Drysdale's *History of the Presbyterians in England*; Trans. Essex *Archæol. Soc. New Ser.* vol. iv. pt. ii. p. 11; Baker's *MSS. Harl.* 7046, ff. 272 d, 292 d; Hunter's *Chorus Vatum, Addit.* MS. 24489, fol. 283, and 24492, fol. 19; Davey's

Athenæ Suffolcienses, Addit. MS. 19165, fol. 520; information from the registers of Dedham per the Rev. C. A. Jones; and from the Leyden *Stadtarchiv*, per C. M. Dory.

The works of Matthew Newcomen:

1. [co-author] *An Answer to a Book entitled, An Humble Remonstrance*; in which, the Original of Liturgy and Episcopacy is discussed: and Queries propounded concerning both. The Parity of Bishops and Presbyters in Scripture demonstrated. The occasion of their Imparity in Antiquity discovered. The Disparity of the Ancient and our Modern Bishops manifested. The Antiquity of Ruling Elders in the Church vindicated. The Prelatical Church bounded. Written by Smectymnuus. 4to. pp. 94. 1641.

2. *Smectymnuus Redivivus...* Composed by five...divines. 4to. 1669.

3. *The All-Seeing Unseen Eye of God*; a Sermon from Heb. 4:13. preached before the Hon. House of Commons, Dec. 30th, 1646, being the day of their solemne monethly fast. 4to. London, 1647.

4. *Another Sermon in the Country Collection*, which is the last in the volume, from Acts 20:32. entitled, Ultimum Vale; or, The last Farewell of a Minister of the Gospel to a beloved people. pp. 78. London, 1663.

The All-Seeing Unseen Eye of God, and Other Sermons

5. *The Best Acquaintance, and Highest Honour of Christians.* A Discourse on Job 22:21. A small book. London, 1668.

6. *The Craft and Cruelty of the Churches Adversaries, discovered in a Sermon on Neh. 4:11*, preached at St. Margarets in Westminster before the Honourable House of Commons assembled in Parliament, Nov. 5, 1642. 4to. pp. 70. London, 1643.

7. *The Duty of Such as would Walke worthy of the Gospel, to endeavour Union, not Division, nor Toleration*; opened in a Sermon from Phil. 1:27 at Paul's, upon the Lord's day, 8th Feb. 1646. 4to. London, 1646.

8. *An Endeavour of making the Principles of Christian religion*...plain and easie. London, 1640.

9. *Jerusalem's Watchmen, the Lord's Remembrancers*: a sermon on Isa. 62:6-7 preached...before both Houses of Parliament, and the Assembly of Divines, upon their solemn Fast, July 7, 1643. 4to. pp. 34. London, 1643.

10. Mr. M. Newcomen his *farewell-sermon* on Rev. 3:3, preached at Dedham in Esses, Aug. 20, 1662. [in *A compleat collection of Farewell Sermons*] 8vo. 1663.

11. *The Necessity and Encouragement, of Utmost Venturing for the Churches Help*...preached to the Honourable House of Commons, on the day of the Monthely solemn Fast, 28 June 1643. London, 1643.

12. *Scripture and Reason pleaded for Defensive Armes: or the whole Controversie about Subjects taking up armes.* In which besides other pamphlets, an Answer is punctually directed to Dr. Fernes Booke, entitled, Resolving of Conscience &c. London, 1643.

13. *A Sermon on Acts 13:36 preached at the Funerals of ...Mr Samuel Collins*, Pastor of the Church of Christ at Braintree in Essex, who exchanged this life for immortality...in the year 1657. 8vo. London, 1658.

14. *A Sermon on Josh. 7:10-11 tending to set forth the Right Use of the Disasters that befall our Armies*: preached before the Hon. Houses of Parliament, at a fast specially set apart,... Sept. 12th, 1644. 4to. pp. 41. London, 1644.

15. *The Upright Protestant*, as he was reformed from the superstitious errours of Popery in the happy reignes of Edward the 6th, Qu. Elizabeth, and King James...and for which this...Parliament will live and die. London, 1643.

THE ALL-SEEING UNSEEN EYE OF GOD

[ORIGINAL TITLE PAGE]

The
All-Seeing Unseen Eye of God

Discovered in a sermon preached before the Honorable House of
Commons; at Margaret's Westminster,
December 30, 1646,
Being the last day of their solemn monthly fast.

By Matthew Newcomen,
Minister of the Gospel at Dedham in Essex, and one of the
Assembly of Divines.

"The eyes of the Lord are in every place, beholding the evil and the
good," (Proverbs 13:3).

"The eyes of the Lord run to and fro throughout the whole earth, to
show himself strong in the behalf of them, whose heart is perfect
towards him," (2 Chronicles 16:9).

*Deus totus oculus est, quia Omnia vides. Torus mamus est, quia Omnia
operator, totus pes est, quia ubiq; est.* August.

Published by order of
the Honorable House of Commons.

London,
Printed by *A.M.* for *Christopher Meredith*, at *the Crane in Paul's
Churchyard.*
1647.

INTRODUCTION

To the Honorable House of Commons assembled in Parliament.

Right Honorable,

God has called you to sit at the stern of this tempest-shaken kingdom; the helm of which God has put into your hands in a very difficult time. Some years now you have been conflicting with cross and boisterous winds and seas, and are not yet in safe harbor. Being called at this time to speak to you, I do not know how to better improve the opportunity for the good of your souls and of the public, than by directing your eyes to that only Loadstar, the eye of God; upon which if you fix, you may from there fetch both light and guidance to steer your course so, as you shall save your souls, and may save the kingdom, so as it does not in *portu naufragium (harbor shipwreck)*. I know you are yet encompassed with rocks and shelves, Scyllas and sirens, temptations on the right hand and on the left, but eyeing this eye of God, will enable you steadily, unappalledly, inflexibly, to shape your course to God's glory, the public good, and your own happiness. Which that you may do, *is the prayer of*

Your servant in the Lord and in his work,

MATTHEW NEWCOMEN

THE SERMON

A sermon preached at the monthly fast, before the Honorable House of Commons, December 30, 1646.

"But all things are naked and open unto the eyes of him, with whom we have to do," (Hebrews 4:13).

That we have to do with God at this time, I am confident we all know. O that we did as well know who and what this God is, with whom we have to do. This Scripture which we have now read, will help us to understand that God is pleased to help *us* to understand this Scripture. In this you have three particulars. The first two particulars concern the knowledge of God. The other concerns the God in whom this knowledge is.

Concerning the knowledge of God, you have here: First, the extent of it, πᾶς all things. Secondly, the quality or kind of it. First, it is a clear or evident knowledge. All things are, γυμνὰ, naked. Secondly, it is a full and thorough knowledge, all things are naked and open, τετραχηλισμένα, before his eyes. Lastly, you have here the God in whom this knowledge is. It is he, αὐτοῦ, with whom we have to do.

The first thing in the text is the *extent* of the knowledge of God, it reaches to all things, πάντα, all things. All things that are in God, and all things that are without God. This refers to *all things*, divine and not divine. All things, angelic or human. Heavenly or earthly. All things good or evil, great or small. Secret or open. All things that have been, or have not been. That are, or that are not; that shall be, or that may be, or that never shall, never can be. All things past, present, future, contingent, impossible, "All things are naked and open unto the eyes of him, with whom we have to do."

This field would be too large for me to travel over at this time, I shall therefore only thrust my sickle into one corner of it, and confine my discourse to that knowledge which God has of men and their affairs, not only because that will be most profitable, but also because that seems to be the very reason why the apostle mentions the omniscience of God in this place, that we might make application of it to ourselves and our own actions, therefore be reminded of what he says, "And no creature is hidden from his sight, but all are naked and exposed to the eyes of him to whom *we must give account (or, of with him we have to do),*" πρὸς ὃν ἡμῖν ὁ λόγος.

That knowledge then, which God has of men and of their ways, I shall endeavor to set before you in these following particulars.

First, God knows every man and woman that ever was, or shall be, God knows them before they are. Even in the womb, even from eternity God knows them, "My substance was not hid from thee when I was made in secret, and curiously wrought beneath in the lowest parts of the earth. Thine eyes did see my substance being yet unperfect, and in thy book were all my members written," (Psalm 139:15-16), and from here it follows, that God fully knows the sinfulness of the state and condition that everyone is born in.

Secondly, God knows all the ways and works of men, from the birth, and from the womb. So, "Doth he not see my ways, and count all my steps?" (Job 31:41). Nor was this God's singular exactness and observation over Job. For, "His eyes are upon the ways of man (any man, every man) and he seeth all his goings. There is no darkness or shadow of death, wherewith the workers of iniquity may hide themselves," (Job 32:21-22), "Great in counsel, mighty in works, for thine eyes are open upon all the ways of the sons of men," (Jeremiah 32:19).

Thirdly, God knows all the speeches of all men. Every word, every syllable that the tongue of anyone mutters or whispers, God knows it, "For there is not a word in my tongue, but Lo, O Lord, thou knowest it altogether," (Psalm 139:4). No man that speaks a word for God, his cause or people, but God knows it. No man that speaks a word against

God, his cause or people, but God knows that too; let it be spoken never so closely, secretly. Enoch tells us that God will at that great day, "execute judgment upon ungodly men, for all their hard speeches which they have spoken against him," (Jude 15). And our Savior tells us that of, "every idle word that men shall speak, they shall give account in the day of judgment," (Matthew 12:36), therefore he knows them all.

Fourthly, God knows not only the ways and the words, but even the thoughts of men, "I know their works and their thoughts," (Isaiah 66:18). "The Lord searcheth all hearts, and understandeth all the imaginations of the thoughts," (1 Chronicles 28:9).

Fifthly, God does not only know the ways and words and thoughts of men present, at that instant, while they are thinking, speaking, and doing these things. But when they are past and forgotten by men, they are still present in the knowledge of God, "Thou lookest narrowly to all my paths, thou settest a print (*a mark, a memento*) upon the heels of my feet," (Job 13:27). "My transgression is sealed up in a bag; And thou sowest up mine iniquity," (Job 14:17). "The Lord hath sworn by the excellency of Jacob, surely I will never forget any of their works," (Amos 8:7).

Sixthly, as God knows all the ways, words, and thoughts of men present and past, so he knows all the ways, words, and thoughts of men that are to come, "Thou understandest all my thoughts afar off," (Psalm 139:2). "I knew that thou wouldest deal very treacherously," (Isaiah 48:8). God knew what Israel would both think and do, when once they came into the land of Canaan, and tells it to them before they ever came there, "For I know their imaginations which they go about, even now before I have brought them into the land of Canaan," (Deuteronomy 31:21). God knew what horrible outrages Hazael would commit when he should come to be King of Syria, and tells him of it, when he could scarcely think there was such villainy in his heart, "God knows not only what men have done, or do, but what they will do," (2 Kings 8:12-13).

Seventhly, God knows not only what men will do, but he knows also what men would do, if they were in such or such cases, upon all occasions, emergent and possible.[1] God knew Abimelech would have defiled himself and Sarah, if he had not withheld him, (Genesis 20:6). God knew the man of Keilah would have betrayed David into the hands of Saul, if he had stayed among them, (1 Samuel 23:12). Here is one that is now a private man, God knows what he would be and do, if he were advanced to the place of public office and authority. Here is one that is linked into a godly family, has gracious

---

[1] *Deus cognoscit non solum qua fieri possunt a singulis, sed etiam qua reipsa fierent, quavis hypothesi facta. Quavis occasione proposita, ha tamen occasiones sunt infinita, imo infinities infinita.*

kindred and company. God knows what he would be, if transplanted into another family. There is one that died in his infancy, God knows what he would have been and done, if he had lived 40 or 50 years. God knows all the ways of men, past, present, future, contingent, and possible.

Eighthly, God knows not only all the ways, words, and thoughts of men, past present, future, possible. But (in the next place) God knows the hearts of all men, "For thou, even thou only knowest the hearts of all men," (1 Kings 8:39). God knows the hearts of all men, what their frame and constitution are, whether they are holy or sinful, sincere or hypocritical; therefore it is said that God in Scripture often searches, and tries, and ponders the hearts of men, "The Lord searcheth all hearts," (1 Chronicles 28:9). I know also, my God, that thou tryest the heart, and hast pleasure in uprightness," (1 Chronicles 29:17). The refining pot is for silver, and the furnace for gold, but the Lord tryeth the heart," (Proverbs 17:3). "The Lord pondereth the heart," (Proverbs 21:2). These three words of searching, trying, and pondering, the Holy Spirit used to set out that full, exact, discerning, critical knowledge, which God has of the frame and temper of men's hearts.

Ninthly, as God knows the frame and temper of all men's hearts; so God knows all the purposes and intentions that are in the hearts of men. In the verse before my text, it is said of the word of God, that it is, "a discerner of the thoughts and intents of the heart," (Hebrews 4:12), καὶ κριτικὸς ἐνθυμήσεων καὶ ἐννοιῶν καρδίας, are properly the secret and inward workings of passions and affections. These are the secret and first workings of men's understandings and apprehensions. Now both the one and the other, God sees them. And therefore that is rendered as a reason why the Word of God discerns them. The Word of God is, "a discerner of the thoughts and intents of the heart, for there is no creature that is not manifest in his sight. But all things are naked and open," even the intents and purposes of men's hearts. These things, says Elihu, God does, to, "withdraw man from his purpose," (Job 33:17).

Tenthly, God knows the inclinations and desires of all men's hearts, "The vile person will speak vilely, and his heart will work iniquity," (Isaiah 32:6). God sees the hearts of wicked men, hankering and propending after their wickedness. His heart will work iniquity, "They come before thee as my people cometh, and they sit before thee as my people sitteth, and they hear thy words, but they will not do them, but their heart goeth after their covetousness," (Ezekiel 33:31). God saw that though they pretended to be devout and religious attenders on his word, yet the bent and bias of their heart was after the world. Their heart was toward their covetousness. And so again God sees how the bent and inclination of his people's heart is towards him, "Thou O Lord knowest me. Thou hast seen me, and tried my heart towards thee," (Jeremiah 12:3). All their inward breathings, and secret lifting up of desire after God, are known to him, "Lord all my desire is before thee, and my groaning is not hid from thee," (Psalm 38:9).

Eleventhly, God knows all the designs and projects of all men's hearts. I mention these as distinct from purposes and intentions, because men's purposes are many times but sudden and slight motions, and of little value with themselves. But designs and projects are deep and elaborate things, and have more study and pains bestowed on them. You shall have a man forging a design, weeks, months, years; and working with that secrecy, that as Alexander said, if he thought his shirt on his back knew it, he would pull it off and burn it. But God knows all these designs and projects are never so deeply laid, and never so closely carried, "He discovereth deep things out of darkness," (Job 12:22). "God will both bring to light the hidden things of darkness, and will make manifest the counsels of the heart," (1 Corinthians 4:5). He, "disappointeth the devices of the crafty, so that their hands cannot perform their work," (Job 5:12). An instance of this you have, (Daniel 11:20-27) where God foretells the several projects and devices by which Antiochus should work himself into the kingdom of Syria, and almost into the kingdom of Egypt, and then (verse

27) how he and Ptolemy, King of Egypt, shall project to overreach one another, "And both these King's hearts shall be to do mischief, and they shall speak lies at one table, but it shall not prosper." As if God had said, after the war between these two kings, there shall be an interview, or a treaty for peace (pretended at least) but there will be nothing but mischief in their hearts; no though they may entertain one another with compliments, and fair words; yet they are but lies and pretenses, they shall both speak lies at one table. God knows all the designs and projects of kings, and great politicians, both in their managing of wars, and in their treaties of peace. In this way you see, God knows all things: all persons, all their actions, all their words, all their thoughts, past as well as present, future as well as past, contingent or possible; all their hearts, all their intentions and purposes; all their inclinations and desires, all their projects and designs. And so you see in some measure the extent of the knowledge of God, all things. The next words will show us the *nature* of this knowledge which God has of all things. It is a clear and distinct knowledge, "all things are marked." It is a full and thorough knowledge, "all things are naked and open." It is an intuitive, comprehensive, infallible knowledge, "all things are naked and open unto his eyes."

First, this knowledge which God has of all things, is clear and distinct. All things are naked. Men may put such colors and dresses on themselves, and ways as they may make a shift to hide themselves from the eyes of men. But no pretenses, no excuses can hide them from the sight of God, no more than a piece of transparent glass can cover them from the beam of the sun, "All things are naked," unmasked, unclothed, their dress and paint taken off. God beholds all things in their naked and simple realities. What a fine color had Simeon and Levi, for their urging circumcision upon the men of Shechem? (Genesis 34:14). They pretended religion and the law of their God; where in truth, it was revenge and thirst for blood that acted them, and God saw this, though Hamor and Sechem did not see it. What a color did Jeroboam put on his idols which he set up at Dan and Bethel, as if he studied nothing but the people's ease, and because it was too far for the people to go up to Jerusalem, therefore he would accommodate them with chapels of ease, (1 Kings 12:2-3). But the naked truth, a design to establish the kingdom to him and his, and to keep the people from returning to the house of David, and this God saw, and so blasted him, that that which he intended for the stability, proved the ruin of his house and kingdom. What a face of zeal for God did Jehu put on in executing the judgment of the Lord upon Ahaz and his family? And when he had done, can vouch warrant from God for it, "This is that which the Lord spake by his servant Elijah," (2 Kings 9:25-36). And can say, Come see my zeal for the Lord of hosts. But God knew it was to rid himself of competitors for the kingdom, and to assure the throne to himself and his, that Jehu did this, and therefore God threatens, "to avenge the blood of Jezreel, on the house of Jehu," (Hosea 1:4), because though he did the thing that God commanded, yet he made the command of God but a color for his own ends. How pious and devout did the Pharisees seem! The people thought they were the only saints on the earth. But our Savior tells them that God looked on them, not according to what they appeared, but according to what they were; their colors, and shows, and pomp of holiness could not blur the eyes of God. So our Savior says, "Ye are they which justify yourselves before men, but God knoweth your hearts; for that which is highly esteemed among men is abomination in the sight of God," (Luke 16:15). Men may be such artificial dissemblers, as not only to be able to justify themselves before men, but to gain a high esteem among them, and yet be an abomination to God, who knows their hearts, and to whom all things are naked.

All things are naked and open: *aperta*, as the vulgar translation has it. *Resupinata*, as Erasmus says. *Intime patentia*, as Theodore Beza says. Chrysostom says, it is a metaphor taken from the skins flayed off from the sacrifices; for as when a man (he says) has slain the sacrifice, and flayed off the skin, all the inwards of the beast are laid open and bare to any eye. So all things, the very inside of them, are naked and open to

God. And Gamerarius approves this explication of the word. Beza carries it further, and says, it is a, "metaphor" taken from beasts, which are not only flayed, but chinned down the backbone; *Ut totae foris & intus ocalis pateant.* So another, *Sicut cum animal per cervicem & spinam dorsi ita dividitur, ut viscera Omnia pateant.* Camero thinks it is a metaphor, *a re palestrich.* Some make the three words in my text, three degrees of the knowledge of God, *videre, denudare, aperire;* a thing may be seen (Athanasius says) but not seen naked; or it may be seen naked, but not open. It is one thing to see a sheep alive with the skin and the fleece on, another thing to see it naked and flayed; and yet a further thing to see it opened. And certainly this phrase signifies a most intimate, full and thorough knowledge of all things, and has the force of that proverbial speech, *intus & incute.*

All things are not only naked, without clothes or colors, but ripped open, emboweled, anatomized, turned inside outward in the eye of God. There is nothing so reserved, so hidden in man or from man, but it is open to the eye of God. Many men have their Arcana, their secret ways of lust which they would not discover, no not to their friend which is as their own soul. But even these are open to God, "Thou hast set out iniquities before thee, even our secret sins in the light of thy countenance," (Psalm 90:8). And there are two things in

27

all men which are hidden secrets, the principles from which, and the ends for which they act; these are like that path of which Job says, "the vulture's eye hath not seen it," (Job 28:7), but even these are naked and open to the eye of God, "All things are naked and open."

"All things are naked and open unto the eyes of him." This shows that the knowledge which God has of all things is not an uncertain, conjectural, fallible knowledge; but a certain, intuitive, infallible knowledge. That it is not an imperfect, successive, potential knowledge, but a perfect, comprehensive, actual knowledge. All things are naked and open to his eyes.

This knowledge which God has of all things, it is (I say) not an uncertain, conjectural, fallible knowledge, but a certain and infallible knowledge; a knowledge that has in it, *evidentiam & certitudinem*. The knowledge of the eye is the most certain and evident knowledge; we say, *visus non fallitur circa proprium objectum*. If the organ and the medium are rightly disposed, a man's eye cannot deceive him; therefore we say, we will believe our own eyes against the entire world. Now God's eye is (as I may also say) both the organ *and* medium of his seeing. We see things by the light of the sun, but the sun sees all things by his own light, so does God. All that is God sees, and God sees all that is, and is not deceived, because he does not need light from without himself to see by, for it is he that sees, and it is from himself that he sees.

Again, this knowledge which God has of all things, it is not a potential, partial, imperfect knowledge, but an actual, comprehensive, perfect knowledge. God with one infinite, undivided act of his understanding, knows at once, all things that ever were, are, or shall be, yes infinite things that never were, nor ever shall be. God does not take up the knowledge of things as we do, *per discursum*, or *per successionem*, or *per conpositionem*. God does not know, *unum post aliud*, one thing after another; nor *unum per aliud*; one thing by another; but his infinite understanding grasps all things, *simul & semel*. To this infinite eye all things are naked and open at one view. God neither looks back on what is past, nor looks forward on what is to come, nor looks right forward on what is to come, nor looks on what is before him immediately, as our manner is; but in a manner far differing from what we are accustomed to do. God does not remove his thoughts from one thing to another, but sees all things altogether unchangeably. God does not see things otherwise with his mind, than with his eye, for he is not made up of soul and body. Nor does God see things otherwise now than he did before, or then he will hereafter; for in God's understanding there are not those differences of time past, present, and to come, as there are in ours; for in his incorporeal view, all things are present together, as Augustine says.[2] The eye of God, my brethren, is not like the eye of man, that cannot see at a distance, or cannot look upon many things at once, fixedly. No, the eye of God sees the remotest things, because he is in all things; the most subtle things, because his eye is sharp, and piercing; the greatest things, because all things are in him. The eye of man may be hindered from seeing, or deluded in its sight, either by blackness of darkness, depth of night, thickness of clouds, alteration of air, distance or place, indisposition of the object or organ, scattering of the species, change of the medium, swiftness of motion, and a hundred such impediments, inward, outward, natural, and artificial. It is not so with the eye of God, who alone by his own infinite and uncreated light chases away darkness, dispels the night, enlightens obscurity, *etc.* His eye is neither hindered by too much nearness, nor by too much remoteness of the object, nor is it wearied with continual seeing. He alone does not borrow his sight, neither from the object nor from the species, nor from light and color, nor from motion. His sight is neither limited to time, nor confined to place, but he sees everything at all times, and in all places; every endeavor, every employment, every wrong, every

---

[2] See Augustine on his view of this in his commentary on Psalm 50.

word, deed, attempt, and thought. All things are (at once) naked and open to his eyes, with whom we have to do.

Of him with whom we have to do. These words set out the person in whom this knowledge is, and that is *he*, "with whom we have to do." The words are diversely translated and interpreted.

The Syriac renders it thus, *of him to whom we must give account*. And this sense Chrysostom gives of the words, *with whom we have to do*, for to him we must give account of what we have done. So then it is worth our considering, that all things are naked and open to the eyes of him, to whom every one of us must give account of himself.

The vulgar Latin reads it, *ad quem nobis sermo*, and so Erasmus and Camerarius, *quem alloquimur, whom we speak to*. And this also is worthy of our consideration. Every time we come to speak to God in prayer, that all things are naked and open to the eyes of him, to whom we are speaking when we are in prayer.

Calvin and Beza render it, *quicem nobis est Negotium*, which is according to our translation, with whom we have to do (Phil. 3:21). The whole life of a Christian is a negotiation with God. Our business *is in heaven*, with God, even then when we think we have to do this or that with some man in business, even then we have to *do with God*. In everything we do, *we have to do with God.* O that we could remember this, and with it remember that all things are naked and open to the eyes of him with whom we have to do.

Others from the connection of this verse with the former, in which the Apostle had been speaking of the ministry of the Gospel, and the efficacy thereof, give this sense of the words, *Deus quicum nobures est, quando cum verbo ejus nobis est, Omnia perspicit.* God, with whom we have to do when we have to do with his word, sees all things. Now, O that we could remember this. That when we have to do with the word of God either to handle, or to hear it, we have to do with God. And with it remember, that all things are naked and open to the eyes of him with whom we have to do.

And it must necessarily be this way. First, because of the infinite perfection of God. God is a being of infinite perfection. All excellence and perfections are in God after a most eminent and infinite matter; and therefore as life, and power, and goodness, and other excellencies are in God, so also knowledge. Which is one of the highest excellences and perfections of life, is in him, in infinite perfection. If there is anything which God did not know, God could not be perfect nor happy in his life and being.

Secondly, this is demonstrated from God's omniscience. God is in all things, and therefore knows all things. God, after an unspeakable manner everywhere, fills all things which he has made; spirits, bodies, things that are above, and things that are beneath, things in heaven, and things in earth, things that have life, and things that have no life. You hold all things, and fill all things, and encompass all things, and are above all things, and sustain all things. Neither do you fill them on the one side, and encompass them on the other, but by encompassing you fill them, and by filling you encompass them. By sustaining them, you are above them, and by being above them, you sustain them. It is necessary that God that so fills all things, and knows all things.[3] Try to imagine in your thoughts, a sphere of infinite greatness and efficacy, whose center is everywhere, but has no circumference; it will necessarily follow that whatever thing or things are, besides this sphere, must necessarily be *within* this sphere, encompassed by it, and contained in it. And all things existing within this sphere it will follow, *nihil agi posse quod ab illa non sentiatur*, there is no action nor motion but this sphere will perceive it. Such is God, a sphere of infinite being, life, understanding, encompassing all things, filling all things, and therefore knowing all things. David proves God to be omniscient from his omnipresence, "Thou knowest my downsitting, my uprising, thou understandest my thoughts

---

[3] *Si animo as mente spharam contemplemur magnitudine ac vurtute infinitam, cujus centrum ubiq, sit, circumserentia nusquam.*

afar off. There is not a word in my tongue, but Lord, thou knowest it altogether," (Psalm 134:2). There is his acknowledgement of God's omniscience. But then, "thou compassest my paths, and my lying down," (verse 3). "Thou hast beset me behind and before," (verse 5), "and whither shall I go from thy Spirit, and whither shall I flee from thy presence?" (verses 7-11). They are acknowledgements of God's omnipresence as demonstrations of his omniscience. And so God himself argues, "Can any hide himself in secret places that I shall not see him, saith the Lord? Do not I fill heaven and earth?" (Jeremiah 23:24).

Thirdly, this omniscience of God is further demonstrated from that influence which God has *into* all things. It is God that gives life, being, motion, power, activity, and action to all things, "In him we live and move and our being," (Acts 17:27). All things that have being, God has given life to them; all things that move, God gives that motion to them, not only the power, but the act; no man can move a hand or a foot to any action; no man can move his tongue to speak a word; no man can move in one thought of his heart, without God's concurrence to that motion. There is no action or motion of any creature, man, or angel, but God concurs to it, by way of support and cooperation as it is a natural action, or motion, by way of special assistance, if it is a gracious and holy action; by way of permission and sufferance, if it is sinful.

Even in our sins, the action, *qua action*, is from God, the ἀνόμοις, irregularity of it is from ourselves. Now this is a further demonstration that God knows all things; and this argument David also uses in Psalm 139:15-16. And so I have finished with the explication of the text, and demonstration of the truth contained in it; I now come to its *application*.

Use 1. The first improvement that I will make of this point shall be for information, "All things are naked and open unto God." God is omniscient; if this is so, then this forms us, that Jesus Christ is God, and the Holy Spirit is omniscient. Omniscience is an incommunicable attribute, and therefore the servants of God from those Scriptures that attribute omniscience to Christ and to the Holy Spirit (as many Scriptures you know do) have successfully and invincibly maintained the deity of Christ and of the Holy Spirit, against the blasphemous oppugners of it, (John 2:24-25, 21:17, Luke 10:12, 12 Corinthians 2:10-11). Chrysostom applies these words of my text to Christ, he speaks of the Son, and says, *with whom we have to do*. I do not speak this as if I suspected any in this auditory guilty of so foul a crime as the denial of the Godhead of Christ, or of the Holy Spirit (though I fear, there is as much of the first blasphemy in England at this day, as ever was since the name of Christ was known in England). But I speak it only to let you see how pious and just it is in the honorable houses, that as they have begun to declare their zeal for God in making a law that men may no longer *impugn* wickedly, and pertinaciously blaspheme his glorious essence and attributes; so to show the like zeal for the glory of his eternal Son and Spirit. This is the will of God, "that all men should honor the Son, even as they honor the Father, he that honoreth not the Son, honoreth not the Father," (John 5:23).

In the days of Theodosius, the Arians through his connivance were grown very bold, and not only had their meetings in Constantinople, the chief city of the empire, but would dispute their opinions; and no man could prevail with the emperor to lay restraints on them, because, the historian says, he thought it *nimis severam & inclemens esse (was very severe and inclement)*; at length he comes to Constantinople, one Amphilochius, bishop of Iconium, to a poor town. He is an honest man but no great politician for the world. He petitions the emperor to restrain the Arians, but in vain. Next time he comes to the court, finding the emperor and his son, Arcadius, (whom he had lately created joint emperor) standing together, he shows very low obedience to the father, but none to the son; but coming close up to him, in a familiar manner strokes him on the head and says, *salve mi fili, God save you my child.* The old emperor taking this for a great affront, being full of rage, bids to turn the man out of doors. As the officers were dragging him forth, he turning to the emperor says, *ad hune modum existima, O imperator. Make account, O emperor, that thus, even thus is the heavenly Father displeased with those that do not honor the Son equally with the Father.* Which the emperor hearing, calls the bishop back again, asks him forgiveness, presently makes a law against Arianism, and forbids their meetings and disputations, *constituta paean.* Here was a blessed artifice, by which the zeal of this emperor was suddenly turned into the right channel. And he was taught by his tenderness over his own honor, and the honor of his son, to be tender over the honor of God and his Son, Jesus.

Use 2. In the second place this, "That all things are naked and open unto the eyes of God," confutes those that say, God does not see, nor know sin. And secondly, that say, God does not see sin in his children.

First, as such say, God does not see sin. God (they say) knows all things by knowing himself, and by looking upon himself, sees all things in himself, *tanquam in speculo.* Now God, they say, cannot see sin in himself, for it is not in him, therefore God cannot see sin. Besides, Scripture says, "Thou art of purer eyes than to behold evil, and canst not look on iniquity," (Habakkuk 1:13). I answer, God does know the sins of men, not as if our sins were represented in the divine goodness, *tanquam in idea,* or *in specula.* But sin being a privation, that (as all other privations) is known by the contrary habit or act, *ut cacti as per visum & tenebra per lumen*; so God knows sin, *per virtutem oppositam & per bonitatem actus opposite.* And as for that text in Habakkuk, it is to be understood, not *descientia simplicis intelligentia*, but *descientia conjuncta cum approbatione. Deus non congnoscit peccata per scientiam approbationis.* And of this knowledge the text speaks. That God *saw* the sins and violences of wicked men, that text tells; and the prophet under a temptation, almost imputed to God an approving of them, which was contrary to his nature, "Thou art of purer eyes than to behold evil, and canst not look upon iniquity, wherefore lookest thou upon them that deal treacherously and holdest thy tongue?"

Secondly, this confutes those Antinomians that say, God does not see the sin of his justified children. Certainly, if all things are naked and open to the eyes of God, then even the sins of his own dearest saints and children God sees. No, say some, by no means; their sins are all *covered.* And the great text they pretend to is that, "He hath not seen iniquity in Jacob, nor beheld perverseness in Israel," (Numbers 23:21). Now it is true, the sins of justified persons are covered. David and Paul tell us so. But with it they tell us how. Not simply and absolutely, so as God cannot see them; this would argue impotency and imperfection in God; but in *secundum quid*, so covered as God will not impute them. And for that which is their *Locus palmarius*, it is never a point to their purpose, "He hath not seen iniquity in Jacob, nor beheld perverseness in Israel," so it is ordinarily read. But a reverent and learned author has with much dexterity and strength proved, it should rather be read, "He hath not seen, or will not see, or cannot endure to see any wrong against Jacob, or any grievance against Israel (for so the words there used often signify trouble and grievance) as he has at large proved from Scripture, and the context exceedingly favors this interpretation.[4]

But take the words in the ordinary reading, they will no way favor this opinion. He has not seen iniquity in Jacob, nor beheld perverseness in Israel, of whom does Balaam speak this? Only of believers, of justified persons? No, of all the hundred thousands of Israel, that were now before him upon the plain; of all the mixed multitude that came out of Egypt, which surely were not all believers, nor justified persons; therefore the meaning of the place is, that at the present there was no common sin lying upon the people, no idolatry (for of that many understand this place) nor any other *peccatum flagrans*, that might provoke the Lord against them (see the Chaldee paraphrase on this). God saw no wickedness in the

---

[4] See Mr. Thomas Gataker in his book, "God's Eye Upon Israel."

camp, that might cause him to pour a curse on them. God saw none, because they had, since their expiation and atonement, committed none, if they had, God would have seen it; for in the 25th chapter, when the people fell to whoredom and idolatry, God could quickly see it and avenge it, and yet the persons remained still the same. These very persons of whom it is said, "God saw no iniquity in them," (chapter 23) within a very few days. And certainly whatever misapprehensions of God and of sin men may now have, the saints of God before us have had far other apprehensions, "O God thou knowest my foolishness, and my sins are not hid from thee," David says, (Psalm 69:5). "Thou hast set our sins before thee, even our secret sins in the light of thy countenance," Moses says, (Psalm 90:10). "If we have forgotten the Name of our God, or stretched out our hands to any false god, shall not God search this out? For he knoweth the secrets of our hearts," the Church says, (Psalm 44:20-21). Does God by his Spirit maintain a war in the heart of his children against their secret lusts, and can God do this, and not see and know their lusts? Does he help his children to see, and loathe, and sigh under their lusts and sins, and can it be imagined that God should cause his children to see that which he himself cannot see? Do the sins of God's children not fall under the counsel and decree of God? Are they not bounded and ordered by God, and shall we say yet, God does not see them?

Use 3. But I come to a third use, and that is, to reprove the great and common forgetfulness of this glorious attribute of the Lord our God. Not to speak of the common sort of men, that are without God in the world, that live more like atheists than Christians, more like beasts than men; but give me a man even among the best of men, that fully believes, considers, remembers, and improves the truth, "All things are naked and open unto the eyes of him, with whom we have to do." Do we when we have to do with God in prayer, remember that all things are naked and open to the eyes of him, *with whom we have to do*? Our preparations, motives, affections, dispositions, aims, are all naked and open to his eyes. Do we remember this? And can we rush upon that duty so unprepared, so inconsiderately? Can we be in the duty, with wandering dead, straightened hearts? We have to do with God in the hearing of his Word, and do we here remember, that all things are naked and open to the eyes of him with whom we have to do? Do we believe, do we remember that the God with whom we have to do, knows why we hear, and how we hear? Sees what thoughts and what affections are stirring in our hearts, while we are hearing his Word. And is it possible we should hear the word with disdain? May the good Lord be merciful to us, that even in those things in which we have to do with God, we forget the eye of that God with whom we have to do, and let our eye slip off from him, whose eye is ever upon us. What do we do then in the common actions of our lives? In our buying, selling, converse with men, and communing with our own hearts? Where is the man that so speaks and so thinks, and so lives continually, as in the eye of that God, to whom all our thoughts, words, and ways are naked and open. Not that we are ignorant of that all-seeing eye of God, which the very heathens had some apprehensions of. And therefore *Seneca* could give this rule, *Sic vive cum hominibus tanquam Deus videat, sic loquere cum Deo, tanquam homines audiant.* So live with men, as if God saw you, so speak to God, as if men heard you. There is something of the notion of this from the light of nature in all our hearts, and much more by revelation from the Word of God. But alas, we know and do not. None of us all live up to the full of our knowledge in this particular, the Lord humble us and pardon us.

Use 4. In the fourth place, this truth that all things are naked and open to the eyes of him with whom we have to do, speaks to us with *terror*. First, to all sinners in general. Secondly, to some sinners more especially.

First, that all things are naked and open to the eyes of him with whom we have to do. How may it fill with terror the heart of every sinner, of everyone that goes on in his trespasses? You know what Job speaks of some sinners, the murderers, the thief, the adulterer, that it is to them the greatest terror that can be, to be discovered in their wickedness, "If a man sees them (he says) they are in the terrors of the shadow of death," (Job 24:17). The same is true in proportion of every other sinner. What sinner is there that has such a heart of adamant, and forehead of brass, as would not be exceedingly troubled, to have all his sins that ever he committed, to have them all immediately published, and laid open before this whole congregation, it would not a little trouble him. Well sinner, this truth tells you that, which if you have not wholly put it off, it will trouble you infinitely more. It tells you that all your wickedness is naked and open to God. It tells you that all your thoughts, all your proud, covetous, unclean, filthy, abominable thoughts; all the thoughts that ever you had in your heart, they are all naked and open to the eye of God. All your oaths, blasphemies, bitter, virulent, malicious, unchaste, unsavory, ungodly speeches that ever fell from your uncircumcised lips. They are all before the eye of God. All your wantonness, luxury, impurities, filthiness not to be named; all your cruelty, oppression, injustice, bribery; all your sins, however secretly contrived and committed, they are all naked and open to the eye of God. Your midnight sins, your closet sins, your curtain sins, your bosom sins, your heart sins, all the sins you have committed, and all the sins you would have committed, they are all naked and open to the eyes of God. *Do you believe this?* If not, you are an *atheist*; if you do, and yet do not tremble, you are....I do not know what to call you. If possible, you are *worse* than an atheist, that believe all your sins to be this day naked and open to the eyes of him with whom we have to do, and yet do not tremble. Do you know, poor man, worm, do you know with what an eye God looks on your sins? It may be, you think, that God beholds your sins as Gallio beheld the Jews abusing and beating Sosthenes before the judgment seat, but Gallio did not care any of those things. And do you think such of God? Let me tell you *then*:

First, God beholds and looks on all your sins with a strict, watchful, observing, censorious eye, "The ways of a man are before the eyes of the Lord, and he pondereth all his goings," (Proverbs 15:21). God so strictly and exactly eyes your sins, as that he knows not only the number of them, but the measure, proportion, weight, of every one of them, "God is a God of knowledge, and by him actions are weighed," (1 Samuel 2:3). God weighs and observes how much willfulness, presumption, contempt of God is in every sin, how heavy and heinous your sins are. That eye of God to which all your sins are naked and open, it is a strict, observing, pondering eye.

Secondly, it is a pure, holy, severe eye, an eye flaming with indignation against every sin, "Thou art of purer eyes than to behold evil, and canst not look upon iniquity,"

(Habakkuk 1:13). Indeed, if God saw your sins with such an eye as men do, it need not much trouble you. Men can see your sins and wink at them; see your sins, and like you, never have the worse done for them. But O if you could see that angry, flaming, revengeful eye with which God sees *all* your sins, it would make your heart even die within you. I have read of Marius and Attilas, and some others, that they have had such fiery sparkling eyes, as that when they have been set upon by enemies, the very sparks of fire darting out of their eyes, has struck such a trembling into the hearts of their assailants, as has made them let their weapons fall. O that you could see with what an eye God looks upon your sins, God has a *revenging* eye. One aspect of this eye of God, is able to make the whole earth to tremble, "He looketh on the earth and it trembleth," (Psalm 104:32), and shall this eye of God be upon you and all your ways, and yet you not tremble?

Thirdly, consider this God, unto whose pure, pondering, severe, revengeful eye, all your sins are naked and open, is the God which will one day judge you for these sins of yours, which his own eye has seen, "For God will bring every work into judgment, and ever secret thing, whether it is good or evil," (Ecclesiastes 12:14). *Ipse autem & Judem erit & Testis.* And he himself will be both the *Judge* and the *Witness*, whom no guilty conscience can escape, for all things are naked and open to his eyes, Augustine says. And again, will God when he comes to judgment, call in witnesses to be informed by them what manner of person you are? How can he be mistaken in judging what you are, who knew before you were, what you would be? God will question you, and not others concerning you, and God will question you, not to get information from you, but to put confusion on you. And, O my brethren, think, I beseech you, how great confusion will fall on every sinner in that day, when the righteous and holy God shall from his own sight and knowledge, convince the drunkard of his drunkenness, the adulterer of his uncleanness, the perverter of the injustice of his bribes, and every other sinner of their several, secret, personal sins. When God shall say to them, as Elisha did to Gehezi, "Went not my heart with thee, when the man turned back from his chariot to meet thee?" So when God shall say to you in that day, "Went not my heart with thee, when thou and thy companions in wickedness met in such and such a place? When you plotted, acted such and such villainies, did I not stand by and look on? O would proud and sinful man think of this eye and this day, how would it make him come down, sit in the dust, and clothe himself with trembling.

In that great, dreadful and strict judgment, we shall stand naked, sorrowful, trembling (Augustine says) the angels and thrones of heaven shall be about us, the books and records of our lives shall be opened, every man presently shall give an account of himself, of all his thoughts, words, actions, of all the sins that he ever committed, by night or by day. This is a judgment (he says) wonderful to see, and dreadful to hear. The thoughts and remembrance of it made such deep impressions on the heart of this holy man, that in another place he says; *Behold in what danger I stand continually, though I do not continually think of it; and the more wretched I, that I can forget it. For God always sees me and all my sins, a strict sentence always awaits me; in this condition I am, when I wake, and when I sleep, when I laugh, and when I am sad; when I am proud, and when I am passionate; Sic sum semper & ubiq, thus I am always and everywhere.* O could sinners when they are in their pangs of pride, passion, mirth, and madness with Augustine, consider themselves as set under the eye of God, whose severe sentence they must abide, it would quell and awe them.

Secondly, this truth, that all things are naked and open to the eyes of him with whom we have to do. It speaks terror as to all sinners in general, so in particular to all hypocrites and dissemblers, that pretend to be much for God, and the Gospel, and religion, and the public good, and all this while, they are but pretenders to these things, and make God and the Gospel and religion and the public good, but serve their lusts and ends; but be as stirrups to get up into their saddle, but as steps by which to mount to their heights. As Jehu made his zeal against idolatry, his breaking down the house, and abolishing the worship of Baal, a pair of stairs to get up into Ahab's throne; as the Pharisees made their strictness in religion, their great devotion and long prayers, but an artifice to insinuate themselves into the people's esteem, and to devour widows' houses. Well, whoever you are, that are guilty in this kind, know it, (and know it to your terror) there is no sinner on earth, whom God hates more than he hates you. For there is no sin that is more directly and formally contrary to the nature of God, who is truth itself, and cannot lie, than this sin of dissembling is. And there is no sin that more either denies or dares this glorious attribute of God's omniscience, than this sin does. Do you think you can easily blur and delude the eyes of God, as you can blind and elude the eyes of men? Can you with all your colors, shows, pretenses, disguises, blind the eyes of God? All things are naked and open to his eye, God sees you as you are, and not as you would seem. Jeroboam's wife thought to have put a cheat on Ahaziah the prophet, because his eyes were dim with age, and he could not see; therefore she disguised herself, and enjoyed herself to be another woman. But God could see, though this prophet could not, and God could tell his prophet who she was, for all her disguise, and the prophet calls her by name, "come in thou wife of Jeroboam, wherefore fainest thou thyself to be another woman," (2 Kings 14:5). Men may so disguise themselves, as they may put a cheat on God's people (yes and prophets too) for their sight is but dim. They may seem saints in the eyes of the most judicious men, and pass with them for others than they are. But God sees you as you are, and God will call you by your name. God will say to you, "come in thou hypocrite, thou pretender, thou manpleaser, thou self-seeker, wherefore fainest thou thyself to be another?" I say to you in the name of God as Paul did to Ananias, "God shall smite thee thou whited wall, thou painted sepulcher." God will wash off all your paint and varnish, all your smoothness and your colors from you, God will discover your filthiness and rottenness even to men, to the loathing of your person. You shall seldom know a gross hypocrite to go to the grave undiscovered.

There is yet another sort of sinners, to whom this truth is matter of trembling. And they are such as drive a trade of projects and designs. And we live in an age that is full of them, never any more. I confess that wisdom is good, it is God's gift. And counsel is necessary. But look to it, that your designs be good, that your consultations be for God, and for his glory. But if any of you are found in a plot or consultation with those of whom the Holy Spirit speaks, "They take counsel against the Lord, and against his Christ," (Psalm 2:2). If any of you drive a design to hinder what God would have promoted, or to promote what God would have suppressed, or divide what

God would have united, or the like; God, who sees and knows the designs that are in all men's hearts, from heaven will blast them. God will cramp you, that your hands shall not be able to perform your work. There is a text very worth our looking on, "Woe unto them that dig deep to hide their counsel from the Lord, and their work is in the dark, and they say who seeth us, and who knoweth us? Surely your turning of things upside down, shall be as the potter's clay," (Isaiah 29:15-16). Where you first have the men described, secondly their misery. The men are described first from the closeness of their plots, "they dig deep," and, "their work is in the dark," and they make account; no man knows what they are plotting, and, "they say who seeth us and who knoweth us?" Nay they do the best they can to hide their designs, not only from men, but from God, "they dig deep to hide their counsel from the Lord." Secondly, they are described from their industry to compass their designs. *Omnem movent lapidem*, they try always, they turn things upside down, to bring about their designs. These are the men here spoken of. The misery and woe here threatened against them is, that they shall lose all their labor, the designs they travail so much with; they shall be as an abortive birth, "Their turning of things upside down shall be as the potter's clay." They look as the potter's clay, when the potter has spent time and pains in tempering and forming it upon the wheel, and now the vessel is even almost brought to its shape, a man

50

that stands by, may with the least push put it clean out of shape and mar all that he has been forming upon the wheel. So (God says) shall all your plots, and all your turning of things be upside down. When you think that you have brought them even to maturity, to perfection, when you look on your business as if it were almost done, God that stands by and looks on, with one touch will dash and mar all. This is the woe that the Lord here threatens against them. And there can be no greater woe upon earth, to a mere politician, than to be baffled and fooled in his designs; when God deals thus with them, he pierces them in the right vein. God has Achitophel, that great oracle of his times, but one such foil as this, and his spirit was not able to bear it, he went home and hanged himself.

In the fifth place. This truth, that all things *are* naked and open to the eyes of him, with whom we have to do. How should it abase and humble every one of us, in the sight of that God before whom we stand, and with whom we have to do this day? That God before whom we stand this day knows all our sins, and knows all our hearts. The sins that we do not know, having committed them through ignorance, he knows them. They have escaped our eye, but they cannot escape the all-seeing eye of God. O God, you know my foolishness, (Psalm 69:5). The sins that we have committed and forgotten, God knows them, they are still present to him, and he is able to present them to us, "I will reprove thee, and set thy sins in order before thee," (Psalm 50:21). God is able, exactly to set before us all our sins, from the first to the last, in the same order in which we committed them, for he fully and exactly knows them all. What we did in our infancy, what in our childhood, what in our youth, what we have thought, or spoken, or did at such a time, and what in such a place, and what in such a company, in the morning, and what at midnight. What you did last night, and what this morning before you came together, and what you have been, and what you have done here, what preparations you have made for these duties, what thoughts and affections you have had in these duties. God knows what raving thoughts, what vile thoughts have been in any of your hearts, how dead and unaffected your hearts have been in confessing, praying, hearing. Now, how should this humble us, and fill our faces with shame in his presence! Were all our sins, and sinful thoughts written this day with a sunbeam (as Tertullian's phrase is) that every man could read and know what we have done, and been, and are, how should we blush in the presence of men? And shall we not much more in the presence of God that knows all things? O let us in humble acknowledgement of our former iniquities, and of this day's sins, everyone of us say with Ezra, "O my God I am ashamed and confounded, and I blush to lift up my face unto thee, O my God," (Ezra 9:6).

And again, "Behold we are before thee in our trespasses, for we cannot stand before thee because of this," (Ezra 9:15).

Use 6. In the sixth place, this truth, that all things are naked and open to the eyes of him, with whom we have to do, may serve to exhort all of us to sincerity, and singleness of heart; to study to approve ourselves to God in all our ways. This is that *unum necessarium (one thing necessary)*, which though neglected and disesteemed by most men, will in the issue be found most comfortable and advantageous, even singleness and plainness of heart. You know what is said of Jacob and Esau; Esau was a cunning hunter, but Jacob was a plain man. Esau, he had his game and his venison, the fat morsels (and much good it may do them) but, believe it, the plain hearted *Jacobs* will go away with the blessing; they will at length prevail with God, and prevail with men. Plain-heartedness will prevail more than ten thousand policies and cunning tricks. Now, to establish everyone in this plain-heartedness, I know a no more powerful and effectual means than the frequent remembrance of the all-seeing eye of God on us, that searches into all the dark and crooked windings of every one of our hearts.

And therefore that is a second thing I would exhort you from this truth to accomplish. To *eye* this all-seeing eye of God, to labor to get our hearts always to set and observe him, who always sees and observes *us*, that we may say with David, "I have set the Lord always before me," (Psalm 16) and, "Mine eyes are ever towards the Lord," (Psalm 25), and there are especially two sorts of men to whom I would commend this *duty:*

First, to kings, princes, rulers, judges, magistrates. They are God's deputies, vice-garents, for them to remember how that God who has committed power and trust to them above other men, has his eye continually upon them, strictly observing how they discharge that trust, and manage that power. O how careful, how exact would it make them? How would it make them impregnable to all corruption, entreaties of friends, respects of blood or brethren? How would it make them administer justice by a true and even balance, without respect of persons? Therefore that good King Jehoshaphat, when he sat Judges over Judah, he gives them this charge, "Take heed what you do, for you judge not for men, but for the Lord, who is with you in judgment (not only to assist you, but to oversee you) wherefore now let the fear of God be upon you, take heed and do it, for there is no iniquity with the Lord, nor respect of persons, nor taking of gifts," (2 Chronicles 19:6). So David, "God standeth in the congregation of the mighty, he judgeth among the gods," (Psalm 82:1). Right honorable and beloved, whom God has called to sit in Parliament, and has placed upon you the highest power and judicature, that this kingdom knows. You have often heard that the eyes of all the people of this kingdom are upon you, that the eyes of these three kingdoms are upon you, that the eyes of all the Churches of Christ are on you, and therefore you had need to take heed what you do; and to do it in truth. So you had, even on that consideration, to take heed of this. But let me now put you in remembrance of that which is more than all this, the eyes of God are *on you*. And let (in the Name and fear of God, I beseech you,) these words sink deeply down into your hearts, the eyes of God are upon you; if you do not prosecute your vows, covenants; engagements to God and men, with your utmost strength and vigor, shall not God search it out? If among you there is any found that are secret enemies to the power of godliness, secret encouragers of any wickedness, either in opinion or practice; perverters of justice, and accepters of persons in judgment, shall not God search it out? "For he knoweth the secrets of the hearts," (Psalm 44:21).

O that you would think of this every time you come up into your house, every time any of you stand up to speak in that honorable assembly; O that you would remember, that all things are naked and open to the eyes of God. Other senates and state assemblies have had mottos written over the doors of their senate houses and council chambers; over the senate house in Rome was written, *Nequid respublica detrimenti capia* *(Nothing in the republic suffers ingests)*. O that over the place where the commons of England sit, might be written, "All things are naked and open unto the eyes of him, with whom we have to do." O that it might be written upon the walls of the chambers where your committees sit. But what do I speak of writing it on walls and doors? O that God would write it by his Spirit, in every one of your hearts, that wherever you are, or whatever you are doing, you might still have this in your actual remembrance, that all things are naked and open to the eyes of him with whom we have to do.

Another sort of men to whom I would commend this consideration, are ministers, preachers of the word. They also are men immediately employed by God, they are his ambassadors. Now, could we, did we continually remember the eye of God continually upon us, how diligent, how abundant would it make us in the work of the Lord! How faithful, how courageous, how unbiased, how above the frowns and smiles of men! This was what made Paul so faithful and uncorrupt in the work of his ministry, "For we are not as many that corrupt the word of God, but as of sincerity, as of God, as in the sight of God, so speak we in Christ," (2 Corinthians 2:17). That which made Paul handle the word so incorruptly, and with such sincerity, was this, he spoke it as in the sight of God. I have heard a story of that holy martyr of Christ Jesus, M. Latimer, that having in a sermon at court in Henry VIII's days much displeased the King, he was commanded next Sabbath after to preach again, and make his recantation. According to appointment he comes to preach, and prefaces to his sermon with a kind of dialog in this manner. *Hugh Latimer*, do you know to whom you art this day to speak? To the high and mighty Monarch, that can take away your life if you offend, therefore take heed how you speak a word that may displease his majesty. But (as recalling himself) *Hugh, Hugh* (he says) do you know from whom you come, and on whose message you are sent? Even the great and mighty God, that is able to cast out both body and soul into hellfire forever, and therefore take heed to yourself, that you deliver your message faithfully, and so comes to his sermon; and what he had delivered the day before, confirms and urges with more vehemence than ever. Sermon being done, the court was full of expectation, what would be the issue of the matter. After dinner, the King calls for Latimer, and with a stern countenance, asking him how he is so bold to preach after that manner? He answered: that duty to God and to his prince had enforced him to it, and now he had discharged his conscience and duty in what he had spoken; his life was in his Majesty's hand. On this the King arose from his seat, and taking M. Latimer off from his knees, embraced him in his arms, saying, he blessed God, "that he had a man in his kingdom, that durst deal so plainly and faithfully with him." Had never a King in England since this time, wanted such a faithful, plain-dealing chaplain, to preach to him, it might have been better with England than it is at present.

Use 7. Seventhly, this truth, that all things are naked and open to the eyes of him with whom we have to do; may serve to admonish us to take heed of sin, every sin however secret and small. For there is no sin so small that God will not, nor no secret that God cannot take notice of it; but all things are naked and open to the eyes of him with whom we have to do. It was the prescript of Epicurious the philosopher to his followers, *ut simper cogitarent vita sua testem aliquem adesse*, ever to think that some or other stood by, as witnesses of every passage of their conversation; and Seneca's counsel to Lucilius, ever to think of himself in the presence of Cato, or Scipio, or Lalius, or some other man eminently virtuous. That by imagining himself under the aspect of so grave and austere an eye, he might be kept from absurdities and indecorums. And sure, there is much in the eye of man, to repress and restrain from sin.[5] A soldier (though wrath and revenge seem to be the proper and essential qualities of a soldier) can bridle his rage, and put up an injury in the presence of his king; such majesty is there in the eye of man; yes there is a kind of authority and awe in the eye of a child.[6] But O this eye of God,

---

[5] *Potest miles coram Rege suo non irasci, ob solam Regia dignitatis eminentiam*, Basil says.

[6] *Maxima debetur pueris neverentia, si quid turpe paras*, Invenal says.

this pure, piercing, flaming, glorious eye of God, could we remember that, and set ourselves under that, O what an awe would it lay on our hearts. I can surely scarcely think, there is any heart under heaven so wicked, but would be awed by that eye of God. You have heard of Paphnutius, and Ephrem Syrus, that converted two notorious and impudent strumpets, only by pressing upon them this consideration of the eye of God. Ah brethren, it is as Paul says, "it is a shame to speak of what things are done of some in secret." Do not many men do that in secret, which if their own father, wife, child, or any other, stood by and looked on, they would not dare to do? Well, God has stood by all the while, and looked on you; he saw your secret adultery; he knows when, and where, and with whom, and with how many you have committed folly. His eye saw you when you thought no eye saw you. Darkness is no darkness to him. If you can find a time when, or a place where God's eye is not upon you, cannot reach you, go there, and sin boldly, sin without fear. But where can you go from God's presence, where can you go from his sight? Read that, "Can any hide himself in secret places, saith the Lord, that I shall not see him? Do not I fill heaven and earth?" (Jeremiah 23:24). A man (Augustine says) when he has a mind to some sin, gets out of public, takes himself to his house, retires from that part of his house which is most exposed to view, into his closet or bed chamber; and yet being afraid to be discovered there, he retreats into his heart, and there pleases himself in contemplative wickedness; God is within your heart, and therefore wherever you flee, God is there, for he is more within you than you are in yourself. Poor soul, there cannot rise so much as one proud, unclean, lustful, covetous, revengeful, vain thought in your heart, but God presently sees it, much less can any of your actual sins be hidden from his all-seeing eye. O how should this make us stand in awe, and not sin! You know what that great monarch Ahasuerus said concerning Haman, when coming in, he found him cast upon the queen's bed on which she sat, "What (he says) will he force the queen, before me, in the house?" There was the killing emphasis in these words, before me; will he force the queen before me? What, will he dare to commit such a villainy, and I stand and look on! O brethren, this is the killing aggravation of every sin, it is done before the face of God. This is what God looks upon, as the great affront and indignity done to him. What (says God) will he be drunk before me? Will he swear, blaspheme before me? Will he be unclean before me? Will he break my laws before me? Ah brethren, to consider the infinite, horrible wickedness that is committed in this kingdom, and that it is all before the eyes of God, that God stands and views them all, God stands and looks on, it would amaze any man, and make him in astonishment cry out, as once the heathen did, *Magne regnator cali, tam lent us audis scelera? Tam lentus vides?* Great God of heaven, can you with so much patience, hear and see such wickedness?

Secondly, this, that all things are naked and open to the eyes of him, with whom we have to do, should admonish us, as to take heed of all sin, so especially and in particular, to take heed of putting off or delaying any part of that service we owe to God, or that duty he requires of us, either towards himself or men, on any pretenses or excuses, how just soever they may seem to men or to our own consciences; for God knows us better than men, better than our own consciences. There is a singular text for this purpose, "If thou forbear to deliver them that are drawn to death, and those that are ready to be slain. If thou sayest, Behold we knew it not. Doth not he that pondereth the heart, consider? And he that keepeth thy soul, doth not he know it? And shall not he render unto every man according to his work?" (Proverbs 24:11-12). In this text is counsel and caution, given to all in their several places, to endeavor with their utmost ability to deliver those that are unjustly oppressed and likely to be ruined, and to take heed that they do not put off this duty from themselves, that they do not seek excuses, and plead ignorance, to say they did not know such a one was in trouble, or if they did, yet they knew that he suffered trouble as a righteous person; for they should know he may have pulled this trouble on himself. Or if they know that too, yet they did not know how to help and succor him. Take heed of such excuses as these, "If thou sayest, behold thou knewest it not," ought you not to have known it? Might you not have known it? Certainly it is the duty of every good Christian in his place and sphere to do as Job did, "I was a father to the poor, and the cause which I knew not, I searched out, and I brake the jaws of the wicked, and plucked the spoil out of their teeth," (Job 29:16-17). It is not enough for you to say, "Behold thou knewest it not." That which you did not know, you ought to have searched out, else you excuse one neglect by a worse one, and assuredly God will find this out, for, "doth not he that pondereth the heart consider it? And he that keepeth thy soul doth not he know it? And shall not he render unto every man according to his work?"

And here, right honorable and beloved, let me in humility and faithfulness direct a few words more especially to you. You know, beloved, and we all know how the good hand of God raised you up to be, "saviors," (Nehemiah 3:27, Obadiah 21) to these kingdoms in a very necessitous time. When these kingdoms were (to keep the language of the text,), "drawn to death, and even ready to be slain," the Lord then raised you up to be saviors to us, to save these kingdoms from present and imminent destruction. And O with what zeal and forwardness did you gird yourselves to this great work! How ready were you to inquire and be informed of all grievances and pressures, public or personal? How wholly did you devote and give up yourselves to understand the estate of the kingdom, and to reform abuses and grievances both in Church and State! And through the good hand of God on your counsels and labors, many particular persons, that were drawn to death, and ready to be slain; yea even buried alive in perpetual exile and imprisonment, have been restored to their lives and liberties. Yes and this whole kingdom has been by you, under God, saved and preserved to that condition in which we are this day. Yet give me leave, honorable and beloved, to set before your eyes and hearts, a sad spectacle of some that are at this day drawn to death, and ready to be slain, who stretch out their craving hands to you, for succor and deliverance. And in the fear of God, and in the bowels of our Lord Jesus, I beseech you to take heed how you turn away your eyes from them, and think another day to say, "Behold we knew it not."

I will not mention those many widows and orphans, whose cries are daily in your ears, and plead their cause more pathetically than I or any else can do. You have done very nobly and justly in putting yourselves into a way of relieving them. Only remember, *Bid day qui cito dat*, "Say not unto thy neighbour, Go, and come again, and tomorrow I will give; when thou hast it by thee,"(Proverbs 3:28).

Nor will I urge you to a compassionate sense of many poor, decayed men, who lie in our prisons rotting (as it were) alive. You have begun already to take pity on their woeful condition, and have appointed a committee to consider of some way for their relief, as may stand with the justice and goodness of this honorable house. Only I humbly pray you, what may be done for these poor creatures, let it be done speedily. Nor will I insist on the complaints of a third sort among us, who are as it were, "drawn to death, and ready to be slain," and they are many honest men, such as those of Zebulon, "who were not of a double heart," (1 Chronicles 12:33), who have singly and firmly adhered to you in all the time of your troubles, and done you faithful service, cheerfully obeyed your orders, and vigorously prosecuted them on their delinquents. Some being vexed and molested with suites in law, having actions of battery and false imprisonment laid on them, others oppressed by their delinquent landlords in their fines and leases, or in the re-demanding of those rents, which they have already paid into the hands of your sequestrators. I know that on complaint, any that are unjustly molested shall find relief at your hands. But in the meantime it is a matter of joy and triumph to your enemies, if they can create a vexation to your friends. And to your friends it is a petty death to be so vexed, for nothing but favoring your service. Might not your wisdom think on some course to check this insolence in delinquents?

But these are but private evils, and they are but some few persons and families that groan under them, for relief at your hands. I will show you kingdoms, nations, dying, perishing, if you do not make haste to succor them.

There is Ireland, poor Ireland, that is drawn to death, that is ready to be slain, that is more than half slain already; that lies bleeding, gasping, ready to give up the ghost. Do we not with trembling hearts expect every day that we may hear that Ireland is dead, perished, lost? I am sure you will not, you cannot say, "behold, we know it not." O then do not make your aid and their deliverance slow. Now God has given you so glorious a conquest over your enemies at home, O let your eyes and hearts be on Ireland, and do something speedily, vigorously, for the delivering of your brethren, that are drawn to death, that are ready to be slain, that are killed all the day long. So shall not the blood of Ireland be required at the hand of England.

There is also another object of your commiseration, and that is England, our own dear England, that has languished of a bloody issue, almost half as long as that woman in the Gospel, till the very strength and vitals of it are almost exhausted. I may say to you of England, as Pharaoh's servants did of Egypt, "knowest thou not that the whole land is destroyed," (Exodus 20:7). I know you have used many means for the gaining of our peace, go on in those endeavors still, and prosecute them now more than ever. And the Lord so bless them with success, that your enemies may see and be forced to acknowledge (what we have affirmed all this while) to wit, that a holy, righteous, safe place, a peace with truth, a peace with reformation, was all you aimed at in your wars.

There is yet another dying object of your pity; and that is truth, religion, the Gospel, the Lord Jesus Christ, that lies bleeding, that is drawn to death, ready to be slain. O do not, I beseech you, forbear to deliver them. There is scarcely any truth of Christ, any doctrine of the Gospel, any point of our religion, but by some temerarious hand or other has been invaded, assaulted, maimed, ready to be slain. The doctrine of the Trinity, of the Godhead of Christ, and of the Holy Spirit, of the verity of the Scriptures; the doctrine of election, of redemption, of vocation, of justification, of sanctification; the work of the Spirit, the rule of life, of holiness; the doctrine of the sacraments, of the immorality of the soul, *etc.* We may say with the prophet Isaiah, "Truth is fallen in the streets," (Isaiah 59:14). And there I think it lies, breathing out David's sad complaint, "I looked on my right hand, and there was none who would know me; Refuge failed me, no man cared for my soul," (Psalm 142:4). I think I see truth and religion lying in the streets, and crying as the poor creatures do that lie by the palace wall, or in the hold at Ludgate, some merciful man have pity on me for the Lord's sake. But as generally neglected and disregarded as those poor creatures are. It is true, right honorable and beloved, that when you first met in Parliament, we were in great danger of losing our religion. There was a popish, Arminian faction, that had a design to rob us of our religion. God gave you hearts to be very sensible of that danger, and to be very zealous for the prevention of it. I, and thousands more, must and will bear your record, that if it had been possible, you would have plucked out your own eyes, rather than have parted with the least apex or iota of divine truth, out of a lenity or indulgence to papist, or Arminian, or any other *heretic*. Where then is your former zeal? Is religion and truth less dear and precious now than it was before? God forbid. Is it in less danger? O that it were. But surely, beloved, our danger in this particular is but a little changed, not quite removed. Then indeed religion was in danger of a more violent and quick dispatch, and now it is in danger of a more lingering, but as sure a death than it was likely to have been dispatched with one thrust of a sword, or one chop of a hatchet, by the hand of known and undoubted enemies. Now it is likely to be stabbed to death with bedkins, with variety and multiplicity of errors, that have wounded our religion in every vein. And this assassination on religion, committed by those that would be counted her chief and only friends. Lift up your eyes and consider; do you not see the body of our religion, lying like the body of Caesar, after he was murdered in the senate house, with above twenty wounds, given him by the hands of his own friends and confederates? Or like the body of Cassianas, whom two hundred of his own school boys stabbed to death with the pins of their writing tables? May we not say of religion, as Prodentius does of that martyr's picture? *Plagas mille gerens, totos lacerata per artus Ruptum mientis pratereas punctis cutem.*

Truly when I behold the face and state of religion among us, it is in my eyes, as if the Lord Jesus Christ were crucified afresh, and put to an open shame in the midst of us. Here comes a blasphemous Arian, and he wounds his head, by denying him to be God. There comes a sectary that is a flat Arminian, though he is not mindful enough to know it, and he wounds him through the heart by maintaining universal redemption, and that Christ shed his blood for all men, a thing that never entered into the heart of Christ. There comes an Antinomian, and he pierces his hands and his feet, by denying that exact walking and working by the rule of the moral law, which Jesus Christ came not to give an indulgence or dispensation from, but to give himself an example of. *Ata hac impune.* Can you plead ignorance of these things, and say, behold we do not know it? You cannot; blessed be God you do not. You have begun to set your faces against these blasphemies and heresies, that (*servis dormientibus*) are broken in on us. Go on in your might, to stop the mouth of all ungodliness, and the zeal of the Lord of hosts be your strength. I know it has been said by some, that because a heart to know and embrace the truth is the gift of God, and the magistrate cannot by forcible means work such a heart in men, therefore the magistrate must use no compulsion or coercion in matters of religion. But certainly, though the magistrate cannot give grace, yet he may compel men to attend on those means where God usually gives that grace, (2 Chronicles 34:23, Ezra 10:7-8). Else you must not only repeal the laws that enjoin papists to come to our churches, but repent of them, as yours and the nation's sins. And though the magistrate cannot give men a heart to know and love the truth, yet certainly the magistrate may make laws to restrain and punish errors and blasphemies that are against the truth. Else, *pari ratione*, because a chaste heart, or a true and loyal heart is the gift of God, and the magistrate by all his penal laws, cannot make men have such hearts, therefore the magistrate may not make laws, to punish adultery, incest, theft, treason. Were this good divinity, or good policy? Go on, go on, right honorable and beloved, do not let such shadows as these stay you. Remember the vows of God are on you, for the extirpation of heresy, superstition, schism, profaneness, and of whatever is contrary to sound doctrine and the power of godliness, as well as of popery and prelacy. Remember, the vows of God are on you, and the eyes of God are on you, and the Lord give you strength so to perform your vows, as you may find acceptance in his eyes. *Amen, amen.*

JERUSALEM'S WATCHMAN

[ORIGINAL TITLE PAGE]

Jerusalem's Watchmen,

The Lord's Remembrancers:

A sermon preached at the Abbey at Westminster, before both houses of Parliament, and the Assembly of Divines, on their solemn fast, July 7, 1643.

By Matthew Newcomen, M.A.
and Minister of the Gospel at Dedham in Essex

"As for me, I have not hastened from being a Pastor to follow thee, neither have I desired the woeful day, thou knowest. That which came out of my lips was right before thee. Be not a terror to me, thou art my hope in the day of evil," (Jeremiah 17:16-17).
"Remember that I stood before thee to speak good for them, and to turn away thy wrath from them," (Jeremiah 18:10).
"Ye that have escaped the sword, got away, stand not still. Remember the Lord afar off, and let Jerusalem come into your minds," (Jeremiah 51:50).

Published by order of both Houses of Parliament.

London,
Printed by *M.F.* for *Christopher Meredith*
August 23 at the *Crane in Paul's Churchyard.*
1643.

INTRODUCTION

To the right honorable Lords, the worthy members of the honorable House of Commons, and the learned and religious divines, now assembled to consult about matters of religion.

This sermon might have been entertained from the pulpit, and now from the press, as Pharez was from the womb, with a *Quam erupisti*, how have you broken forth? Were it not known to this assembly, that the parliament had designed another, both in years and all intellectual and spiritual abilities, far more fit for the solemn work of so solemn a day, in so solemn and reverent an assembly. But bodily infirmities compelling him with Zarah to draw back his hand, the work was (I do not know by what providence) devolved on me, I was to that *quire* of mourners, and intercessors, but as the grasshopper was to Eunomius his harp; *quae Citharae jugo infidens ruptae chordae sonum expleret.*[7]

The same authority (which I am resolved to obey, *usque ad Aras*) that commanded me to preach then, commands me now to make public to the eyes of all, what then was

---

[7] The hearers consisted of both Houses of Parliament, and the Westminster Assembly of Divines all joining in humiliation and prayer.

committed to the ears of not many; when the same Authority shall command other things that have since been spoken and transacted in your assembly to see the light, I do not doubt that all sober minded men that have not been made drunk with the cup of Rome's fornication, will acknowledge that you have with a single eye sought truth with peace, and union with *reformation*.

It is (men, brethren, and fathers) a great work that God has called you to set your heads, hearts and hands to, to rescue truth from the jaws of those monstrous errors that had almost devoured it; to disburden the worship of God of those corruptions, that have so long clogged and defiled it; to advise of, and propound such a government in the Church, as may be most agreeable to God's word, most conformed to the pattern in the mount, and to the practices of the best *reformed* Churches; *Had our God cast you on this work in the most pacate times,* and *among a people,* the most prepared for reformation that ever were, yet (in itself considered) such is the infinite weight of your employment as might even swallow up all your thoughts. But then to consider how unprepared the hearts of people are for which is the work of this age, and this assembly, reformation, which had been represented to both prince and people under the odious notion of Brownism, Anabaptism, church anarchy, confusion; in so much that with many endeavors and assays of reformation will find no better entertainment than Hezekiah's messengers of reformation did, (2 Chronicles 30:10). This is when the people laughed them to scorn and mocked them. No, with some worse, for some burn so enraged after their idolatrous ways, and they are so mad on their own inventions, that if they are denied these, it is to be feared that you will find them in the temper that the Abezrites were, scarcely anything will pacify them, but the blood of those that cast down the altar of Baal, and cut down the grove that was by it, (Judges 6:30). Do not multitudes cry already on the disuse of some ceremonies, and the displacing of some superstitious priests? Do they not cry with Micah, "Ye have taken away our Gods and our priests, and what have we more?" (Judges 18:24). This makes the times so calamitous, as we may say of them with the learned *Rivet*. All this proclaims the work of reformation the more necessary, but with it the more difficult.

Against the difficulties, what do you have to encourage you? Were you encompassed as Elisha sometimes was, with a host of armed men, yet might you say as he did there, "They that be with us are more than they that be against us."

For first, with you are all the armies in heaven. All the saints and Churches of Christ are with you, striving with you by their prayers, (Rev. 19:14, not only in reference to your persons, but to your employments) for protection, guidance, and blessing. The appearing of Christ in the beauty of reformation among us may be said to be the desire of all Christian nations.

Secondly, not only so, but you have the prayers of those that have been before us. For very many prophets and righteous men have desired to see the things which you see, and have not seen them;[8] a parliament resolved on a more thorough reformation; an assembly called to debate and advise about the establishing of doctrine and worship, and the government of the Church in a more pure and regular manner; with how many tears and prayers did our forefathers seek this at the hands of God? The first fruits of which prayers we (who are entered on their labors) have already tasted, and shall reap in full answers, in due time if we do not faint.

Thirdly, you have the promise of our Lord Jesus Christ, "Where two or three are met together in my Name, there am I in the midst of them," (Matthew 18:20). To be met together in the Name of Christ, implies three things: 1. *Convenire ex vocatione (Adapted from the calling). 2. Convenire animo sequendi prasescriptum Dei (Agree to follow the Spirit of God). 3. Ita ut unusquisque diffidat sibi, and soli Deo sidat (So that each one has no confidence in himself, and only God).* And if ever any in all these particulars were met together in the Name of Christ, then are

---

[8] Camero in Myrothce.

you, and therefore may with a holy, humble confidence challenge this promise of our Lord Jesus, to be in the midst among you. Christ, being in the midst of you, implies not only his *adesse (presence)*, but his *praesse (rule)* too. As Psalm 82:1, "And if God be thus with us, who can be against us?" (Romans 8).

Fourthly, some sweet, encouraging, engaging experiences we have had of the accomplishment of this promise. He must have a heart more ignorant and unbelieving than the apostle's idiot, that should come in and be ear-witness of your proceedings and not worship God and report, *That God is in you of a truth.* Verily, I have often from my heart, wished that your greatest adversaries and traducers might be witnesses of your learned, grave, pious debates, which were able to silence, if not convert malignity in itself.

Go on in your might, "hath not the Lord sent you? Is not the Lord with you?" (Judges 6:14). Go on in this your might. *Pergite quo coepistis pede (You began to go to the foot).* In that Spirit of wisdom, love, and zeal for truth, in which you have proceeded here, go on still, to love the truth and peace. Peace is precious, and so is every grain and selvage of God's truth. It was a saying of Basil. And it well resembles him, *qui sacris literis innutriti sunt, ne unicam quidem syllabam divinorum dogmatum prodere sustinent, sed pro his Omnia, si opus sit genera mortis libenter subeunt, (who are brought up to Holy Scripture, indeed not a single syllable of the divine physicians of no value to betray, they endure, but for them all kinds of death gladly if need be, they advanced.).*

The Lord strengthen your hands and hearts to the great work that lies before you, raise you above all discouragements and oppositions, fill you more and more with a Spirit of wisdom, discernment, resolution, courage, zeal, faithfulness; make you in this work of reforming his Church as Zechariah and Haggai were in rebuilding the temple, *ut Ecclesiam hanc, quam invenistis minus quam lateritiam, reddatis plusquam marmoream, (to this church, which we found less than brick, return more than marble)*: which is the sincere desire and prayer of him,

Who is less than the least of all God's mercies and employments,

Matthew Newcomen

THE SERMON

A sermon preached before the Assembly of Lord, Commons, and Divines, on their fast, July 7, 1643.

"Ye that make mention of the Lord keep not silence; And give him no rest, till he establish, and till he make Jerusalem a praise in the earth," (Isaiah 62:6-7, latter part).

Beholding the face of the Church in this chapter, it appears to me as the garden of God, made glad with four precious, gracious promises, like the four rivers that watered the Eden of the Lord, (Genesis 2:1).

1. In the first, the Lord promises to raise his Church out of a low afflicted estate, into an illustrious, glorious condition, "For Zion's sake I will not hold my peace, and for Jerusalem's sake I will not rest," (for so with a learned expositor *Sculteus*, I take the words to be the words of God *promising*, and not of the prophet *saying*), "*For Zion's sake I will not hold my peace, etc.* until the righteousness thereof go forth as brightness, and the salvation of it as a lamp that burneth;" which righteousness shall be so glorious that all the kings and nations of the earth shall behold and admire it, (verse 2), "It shall be as a crown of glory and a royal diadem in the hand of

God," (verse 3). And a new name breathing nothing but delight and pleasure will God put on his Church, because the, "Lord God delighteth in her," (verse 4-5).

2. In the second place, the Lord promises to raise up unto his Church instruments fit for himself to use in this great work of restoring his Church and making it glorious, "I have set watchmen on thy walls, O Jerusalem, which shall not hold their peace night nor day, ye that are the Lord's remembrancers," (verse 6-7).

3. In the third, the Lord promises to continue this his Church's felicity, and confirms this promise with an oath, "The Lord hath sworn by his right hand and by the arm of his strength, surely," (verse 8-9).

4. In the fourth, the Lord promises an increase and dilatation of his Church, by means of this prosperity and glory, "Go through, go through the gates and prepare ye the way of the people, etc. Lift up a standard for the people," (verse 10-12).

Our text lies in the second part of this chapter, in which the Lord having promised to his Church instruments and means fit for himself to use in the effecting of the great things before promised, "I have set (for I will set, a usual Hebraism, thereby to show the certainty of the thing promised) watchmen on thy walls, O Jerusalem." And having undertaken for the fidelity and sedulity of these watchmen, which shall never hold their peace night nor day. Presently by an apostrophe he turns to these watchmen, and gives them a charge to see that they make good what he had undertaken: "Ye that make mention of the Lord, keep not silence; give him no rest, till he establish, and till he make Jerusalem a praise in the earth."

In the words you may be pleased to consider these three *things:*

First, the persons called upon, deciphered in this way, "ye that make mention of the Lord." Here we begin dividing the text.

Secondly, the service or employment they are called to, described negatively, "keep no silence, and give him no rest."

Thirdly, the duration or extent of this employment, "till he establish, and till he make Jerusalem a praise in the earth."

For the first of these, the persons called on, they are in this way characterized, "ye that make mention of the Lord;" the marginal note in our Geneva Bible reads it, "ye that are the Lord's remembrancers." The vulgar, *qui reminiscimini domini. Pagninus, qui reminiscimini Jehova. Arias montanus, Rememorantes Dominum. Jun & Trem. Qui commemorates Jehovam.* All which, unless it is our marginal reading, imply no other than what is the common duty and disposition of all the people of God, to, "remember the Lord, and make mention of the Lord;" only that, "The Lord's remembrancers" seem to have something in it peculiar to some rank and order of men, "ye that are the Lord's remembrancers;" you to whom *ex officio* belongs, to put the Lord in mind of his people and of his promises. In the original it is הַמַּזְכִּרִים שֹׁמְרִים (Isa 62:6) where it says the Kings of Judah and Persia had *suos Maskirim admonitores, qui singular gesta & gerenda Regi in mentem revocarent (2 Sam. 8:16, Jehosephat son of Ahilud;* the word, "recorder" in this verse is the word, "remembrancer"); such as we are accustomed to say are *Regi a commentariis.* It seems this was some standing office in the court to be the King's *remembrancers;* you to whose office it belongs to put the Lord in mind of his Church's necessities, and his promises, which can be no other than the watchmen spoken of in the foregoing words, "I have set watchmen on thy walls O Jerusalem;" therefore the Greek translation joins these watchmen and this remembering the Lord in construction together, "And on thy walls O Jerusalem I have set watchmen all the day, and all the night, which shall not hold their peace forever remembering the Lord;" so that the Lord's remembrancers *here* are the same with Jerusalem's *watchmen* before, and they are no other but the priests and prophets and ministers of the Lord.

The second thing considerable in the text is, the employment they are called to, and that is described negatively, "keep no silence, give him no rest;" which implies that their employment here is vocal, and that can be but either in preaching or in praying. Some think the ministers of the Lord are here called on for diligence in both these; but in this place I conceive, the Lord calls them to attendance on prayer, because of the following words, "give him no rest." The pronoun there having reference to *God*, and not to Jerusalem; keep no silence, give him, that is, the Lord, no rest, pray, cry importunately, and do it incessantly. God here by his prophet calls his ministers to pray, as elsewhere he does, by his apostle, to preach, "in season and out of season;" night and day, "I have set watchmen on thy walls, O Jerusalem, which shall not hold their peace night nor day; ye that are the Lord's remembrancers, keep no silence, give him no rest."

The third and last thing considerable in the words is, the duration or extent of itself, or how long they must continue praying, "Even till he establish, and till he make Jerusalem a praise, until God has not only laid the foundations, but set up the pinnacles of a glorious Church. Not only brought forth the Cornerstone, but the top stone of Jerusalem, and all the earth with shouting, cry, grace, grace to it," (Zechariah 4:7).

I might out of the words present to you several doctrines; as many in number as the parts of the test. *As,*

First, that God will certainly establish Jerusalem, and make it a praise in the earth. This is clear, for certainly God would never call his servants to pray for that which he never intended to do; were there never a text but this in all the book of God, that told us of this beauty and glory with which God in the latter days will clothe his Church, even on earth; were there nothing said of it elsewhere in this evangelical prophet Isaiah; nor any mention of it in that prophetical evangelist St. John, if in his whole book of Revelation, he had not uttered one word of this, the Church's glory. Yet in this one text, there is enough to support the faith of God's people, in the patient and comfortable expectation of it. God has commanded prayer for it; therefore God will do it. For, "He never saith to the sons of Jacob, Seek ye me in vain," (Isaiah 45:19).

Secondly, we might observe that, though the Lord will certainly make his Church glorious, a praise on earth, yet he will not do this until it is obtained of him by earnest and incessant prayer. Therefore, in order to his own holy and blessed ends, he here commands his servant's prayers.

Thirdly, we may observe this, that it is in a special manner the duty of God's ministers to pray earnestly and incessantly to God, that he would establish and make Jerusalem *a praise in the earth.*

This third point I will embrace as adequately answering this auditory and day. To an assembly of God's ministers meeting together in a solemn day of prayer, to seek God for the good of Jerusalem, what can be more apposite than such a doctrine as this that tells them, "It is in a special manner their duty to pray," opportune, importune, incessantly, importunately, that God would establish and make Jerusalem a praise in the earth? The God of wisdom and grace who directed the thoughts of his servant unto this word, enlarge his own gracious hand, and the heart and mouth of his poor and most unworthy instrument, that helped by his Spirit, and your prayers, I may utter right things, and such as may advance God's glory, and further all our hearts, not only in the work of this day, but in that great employment whereunto we desire this day to sanctify ourselves.

DOCTRINE: It is in a special manner the duty of God's ministers to pray that God would establish Jerusalem and make it a praise in the earth.

I will not say, it is needful (in such an auditory, it cannot be) but it may be convenient, and I must *pro more*, a *little open* the terms of this proposition. Not to speak of the persons, on whom this duty is imposed, God's ministers; nor of the duty imposed on them, prayer; I shall only speak of the subject of the duty here propounded to us, which is twofold.

Subjectum cui, or *cujus*; and *Subjectum quod.* The first, showing *whom* we must pray for; and second, *what* we must pray for.

For the first of these, the *Subjectum cui,* or *cujus*, whom we must pray for, the text and doctrine tells us, *Jerusalem.* Jerusalem may be taken two ways, either literally, or mystically.

Literally, for the place and city so denominated, or for the people sometime inhabiting that place. For the place or city, that was for sometime so famous among the nations, the city where God dwelt, the habitation of his holiness, the place near unto which Christ was born, in which he conversed, manifested the truth of his godhead in his actions, the truth of his manhood in his passions, was betrayed, scourged, reviled, condemned in it, crucified, buried near to it, this is literal Jerusalem, (John 19:4). But this is not that Jerusalem we must pray for, our devotions must not with the papists dote on the ruins and rubbish of that bloody city, the city of God's curse.

Secondly, Jerusalem literally signifies the people of Jerusalem, the nation of the Jews, whom God has in his righteous indignation scattered over the face of the earth, as chaff before the wind. These we must pray for, I mean the remnant according to the election of grace, that God would gather them again according to his promise: "And so all Israel shall be saved," (Romans 11:26).

But yet this is not that Jerusalem here meant neither. The Jerusalem meant in this place is the mystical Jerusalem, that Jerusalem, of which this was but a type, the new Jerusalem coming down from God out of heaven.[9] And so it implies *two things*:

First, the Church of God in the utmost latitude of it. The whole Catholic Church dispersed over the world, "the general assembly and Church of the first born is unto us Mount Zion, the city of the Living God, the heavenly Jerusalem," (Hebrews 12:22-23), for which we are to pray that God would establish and make it a praise in the earth. And secondly, by Jerusalem mystical we are to understand that particular Church, in which we live, of which we are, to which we stand in the same relation that the Jews did to Jerusalem; for this we are to pray that God would establish, and make it a praise in the earth. And so I come to the second

---

[9] Revelation 21:2, which text seems to refer to this passage we look at in Isaiah, and speaks the same language. For in verses 4-5 God says, "And God shall wipe away all tears from their eyes; and there shall be no more death, neither sorrow, nor crying, neither shall there be any more pain: for the former things are passed away. 5 And he that sat upon the throne said, Behold, I make all things new. And he said unto me, Write: for these words are true and faithful," (Rev 21:4-5). So here John sees this Jerusalem prepared as a bride adorned for her husband.

thing to be explained, the *subjectum quod*, or, what it is we are to pray for.

Two things we find mentioned in the text. First, that God would *establish*. Secondly, that God would make his Church *a praise in the earth*.[10]

First, that God would establish his Church; for though the Church has a strong foundation, and walls, and bulwarks strong, yet it is in itself but a weak building, earthly tabernacles planted on a rock, (Matthew 16:18; Isaiah 16:1; 2 Corinthians 5). That which God speaks of the earth, may be applied to the Church, "The earth, and all the inhabitants of it are dissolved, I bear up the pillars of it," (Psalm 75:3). All the commissures and consignations of this great fabric of the universe would be loosened and disjointed, if God did not put under his everlasting arms, and bear up, and establish the pillars of it. So would it be in the Church of God; therefore we must pray that God would establish his Church, and that in two things: in truth and in peace. First, in truth against all error; secondly, in peace against enemies.

First, we must pray that God would establish his Church *in truth*. The Church is said, "to be the pillar and ground of truth," (1 Timothy 3:15); not as the papists affirm, as

---

[10] See Jeremiah Burroughs work which was been recently republished by Puritan Publications called, "Jerusalem's Glory Breaking Forth Into the World."

if truth were grounded on the *judgment* and *determination* of the Church. The Church is indeed the pillar of truth, not because it holds up the truth, but because it holds forth the truth; the metaphor is taken, not from pillars that are supporters of houses, but from such pillars as anciently were accustomed to be fixed in marketplaces, and other places of public meeting, on which they hung their laws, (as the *leges* 12 *Tabularum* at Rome) that they might be public to the view and notice of all men; as amongst us proclamations, for the same end are pasted on posts. Such a pillar of truth we grant the Church is, and ought to be a pillar to hold forth the truth, to the view of all men. It should be a pillar to which all men resorting may read, and know the truth; it is *the pillar and ground of truth*; the words in the original are στῦλος καὶ ἑδραίωμα τῆς ἀληθείας. (1 Tim. 3:15), which in the first and native signification is a *seat*; the pillar and seat of truth, the place of truths abode and residence, its proper *ubi*, where truth is always to be found; this the Church of God is or ought to be.

Now, though the Church of God *should be* seen in this way, yet we know there is no Church except that which is subject to error. The apostle tells us there *must be* heresies, (1 Corinthians 11:19) δεῖ γὰρ καὶ αἱρέσεις ἐν ὑμῖν εἶναι, and our Savior tells us that there shall arise some such subtle masters of heresy, that, "they shall seduce (if it were possible) the very elect of God," (Mark 13:22). Therefore, we must pray that God would establish his Church in truth against all errors. Truth is the Church's girdle, (Ephesians 6:14); a Church *qua hane Zona perdidit aut solute est*, as the Latin proverb is, a Church that has lost this girdle of truth, or has this girdle loosed, is an adulterous, beggarly Church; therefore, "ye that are the Lord's remembrancers keep no silence, give him no rest till he establish his Church in truth."

And as in truth, so secondly, in *peace*. Peace is one of the richest blessings of heaven, a comprehensive blessing, a circle of blessing; I will not rhetoricate in the praises of it. The lack of peace has made us know what peace is worth; in the enjoyment of this rich, desirable blessing, we must entreat the Lord to establish Jerusalem, his Church, "ye that are the Lord's remembrancers, keep no silence, give him no rest, till he establish Jerusalem in peace."

And this peace is *threefold*; Civil, with the nations; Ecclesiastical, with its own members; and spiritual or celestial, with its head and God.

First, we must pray that God would establish his Church in peace among the nations; the Church of God is among the nations, as the, "lily among the thorns," (Song of Solomon 2:2). The lot of Israel was among the uncircumcised heathens; so is the Churches; yet the church has her God promising peace in the midst of enemies, "He shall judge among many people, and rebuke the strong nations afar off, and they shall bear their swords into ploughshares, and their spears into pruning hooks, nation shall not lift up a sword against nation, neither shall they learn war anymore, but they shall sit every man under his vine, and under his fig tree, and none shall make them afraid. For the mouth of the Lord of hosts hath spoken it." You that are the Lord's remembrancers, keep no silence, give him no rest, till he establish Jerusalem in peace.

Secondly, there is peace ecclesiastical, peace of the Church with its own members, peace in the bowels and bosom of the Church. We must pray that God would establish his Church in that; that the Church may not languish, and die of Antiochus' disease, a torment in her bowels, that there may be no incomposable divisions, no irreconcilable rents, no incurable ruptures in the Church, which is one of the greatest and saddest mischiefs, and miseries which can fall on the Church, or the Church fall under. That God who makes men to be of one mind in a house, as the Greek reads that of the 68th Psalm, ὁ θεὸς κατοικίζει μονοτρόπους ἐν οἴκῳ, that God can make men of one mind, in a Church, in a nation, in Jerusalem, and has promised that he will do it, "I will give them one heart," (Ezekiel 11:19), and, "I will turn to the people a pure language, that they may all call on the name of the Lord to serve him with one consent, (Zephaniah 3:6). O happy, happy we, if God would fulfill these promises in us! Happy we, if we could obtain this at the hands of God by our prayers!, "Ye that are the Lord's remembrancers, keep no silence, give him no rest, till he establish his Church in this peace."

Thirdly, there is spiritual or celestial peace, peace between God and his Church; we must pray that God would establish his Church in that also, that God would so watch over, and work in his Church, that no sin may take hold and spread on it, which might cause a quarrel between his Church and him, or cause the Lord to say, "Mine heritage is to me as a speckled bird," (Jeremiah 12:9). That God would so order all the ways of his Church before him, and towards him, that he may never know her by any other than those precious and lovely names of Ammi and Ruhama, Hephzibah and Beulah: "Ye that are the Lord's remembrancers, keep no silence, give him no rest, till he establish his Church in this peace also." So you see the first thing we are to pray for, that God would establish his Church on the two pillars of truth and peace, as Solomon did the porch of the temple on those two brazen pillars Jachin and Boaz.

Yet there is one thing more that this text commands us to pray for, that is, that God would make Jerusalem a praise, "Ye that are the Lord's remembrancers, keep no silence, give him no rest, till he establish and till he make Jerusalem a praise in the earth." In the former we pray that God would beautify his Church; make it clear as the morning, fair as the moon, glorious as the sun, terrible as an army with banners, lovely as Tizrah, comely as Jerusalem, the praise of all the earth.

Now God makes his Church a praise in the earth, specially by these *five things*:

1. By furnishing his Church with fullness of ordinances.

2. By ruling his Church according to his own orders.

3. By filling his Church with abundance of light and knowledge.

4. By improving this knowledge to the working of holiness.

5. By enlarging and increasing his Church by these means.

First, God makes his Church *a praise* in the earth, by furnishing it with fullness of ordinances. This was that which was the τὸ περισσὸν, as the apostle calls it, (Romans 3), the preeminence of the Church of the Jews above all other nations, first of all and chiefly, it was this, that to them were committed the oracles of God; this is that which God himself tells his people, should make them glorious and praiseworthy in the eyes of all the nations of the world, "This is your wisdom and your understanding, in the sight of the nations, which shall hear all these statutes, and say, surely this nation is a wise and understanding people. For what nation is there so great, who hath God so nigh unto them, as the Lord our God is in all things, that we call on him for? And what nation is there so great, that hath statutes and judgments so righteous, as all this law, that I set before you this day?" (Deuteronomy 4:6-8). Now when God bestows his oracles and ordinances on a people, first his Word, and then appending ordinances, seals, Sabbaths, censures, administered in purity, and in power, then he makes them a praise: "Ye that are the Lord's remembrancers, keep no silence, give him no rest, till he thus make his Church a praise."

Secondly, God makes his Church a praise by ruling it according to his own order: ατάξιν (disorder) and ἐθελοθρησκία (self-willed religion) are the two great destroyers of the Church of God; it is equally prejudicial to the Church, not to be ordered at all, as to be ordered after the lusts and wills of men; God (who is the God of order, and not the author of confusion, but of peace, as in all the Churches of the saints, (1 Corinthians 14:33)) would have all things in all Churches, "be done decently and in order," (verse 40), now when all ordinances and offices are administered in the Church according as God has ordered, then is that Church a praise in heaven and earth, with God and the saints, "Now I praise you brethren that you remember me in all things, and keep the ordinances as I delivered them unto you," (1 Corinthians 11:2). And on the other side, disorder or deflection from the rule of Christ, though but in one administration, is a blemish and detracts from the Church's praise, as appears in the same chapter, "Now in this that I declare unto you, I praise you not that you come together, not for the better, but for the worse," (verse 17), and, "What, have you not houses to eat and to drink in or despise you the Church of God, and shame them that have not? What shall I say to you? Shall I praise you in this? I praise you not," (verse 22); one aberration from the rule of Christ in the administration of this one ordinance of the supper of the Lord, casts a cloud on this Church's glory, and causes a great diminution of their praise, therefore we must pray that God would help his Church in all things to, "keep the ordinances as they are delivered unto us:", "Ye that are the Lord's remembrancers, keep no silence, give him no rest, till he make his Church thus a praise."

Thirdly, God makes his Church a praise when he fills it with abundance of light and knowledge; when after a night of ignorance or error that had swallowed up, and buried the Church of God, the Church has a resurrection, and looks forth as the morning, clear as the sun, fair as the moon, it ravishes all eyes, and fixes them on itself in admiration, that men say, "Who is this that looketh forth as the morning?" (Song of

Solomon 6:10). "Ye that are the Lord's remembrancers, keep no silence, give him no rest, till he make Jerusalem thus a praise;" remember him of that which he has promised, "All the earth shall be filled with the knowledge of the Lord, as the waters cover the sea," (Isaiah 11:9).

Fourthly, God makes his Church a praise, by improving and sanctifying this knowledge, to the working of holiness in the hearts and lives of his people; this was the praise of Jerusalem, it was a holy city, this is the praise of the Church, they are a holy people, "The Lord hath avouched thee this day, to be his peculiar people, as he hath promised thee, and that thou shouldest keep all his commandments. And to make thee high above all nations which he hath made," (Deuteronomy 26:18-19) and that, "thou mayest be an holy people unto the Lord your God as he hath spoken." Abundance of light unsanctified would make the Church, if it were possible, rather hell than heaven, and make men but like the devils, who know much, but are the more desperately wicked. Therefore, we must pray that God would sanctify that knowledge, by which he fills his Church, so that the beauty of it may be perfect, "Ye that are the Lord's remembrancers, keep no silence, give him no rest, till he make Jerusalem thus a praise."

Fifthly, God makes his Church a praise by increasing his Church, by enlarging the tents, and tending the cords of it;

this is a blessing God calls his Church to rejoice in, "Sing O barren, and break forth into singing, etc. enlarge the place of thy tent, and let them stretch forth the curtains of thine habitations, spare not, lengthen thy cords, and strengthen thy stakes, for thou shalt break forth on the right hand, and on the left. And thy seed shall inherit the Gentiles, and make the desolate cities to be inhabited," (Isaiah 51:1-3). We are to pray that God would make his Church a praise in this way also.

So you have, (Right Honorable, Honorable Reverent, and beloved in our Lord Jesus) the sense of this doctrine as fully as my weak thoughts in the little time I had to bestow on this work were able to comprehend it; you see for whom we are to pray, Jerusalem, the Church of God in general, and our own in particular; you see what it is that we are to desire for the one and for the other, truth, peace, and praise; such a trinity of blessings, as the blessed Trinity has none better to bestow on earth. I know I speak to an auditory so rational as I shall not need confirm this truth by reasons; and to so cordial to the Church of God, as I shall as little need to stir you up to the practice of this truth by application; else I might fill up a large portion of the time remaining in telling you how all the Lord's remembrancers in all the ages of the Church, under the law, under the Gospel, have exemplified this truth. Under the law, before the captivity, Moses, Samuel, David, Isaiah, Jeremy, which of the Lord's prophets have not made the establishing and beautifying of Jerusalem the burden of their prayers? In the captivity though they had lost their urim and thummim, and the fire of the sanctuary that came from heaven, yet they had not lost this holy heavenly disposition, of praying for Jerusalem; see abundant evidence of it in Ezekiel, Daniel, Mordecai; and after the captivity, in Ezra, Nehemiah, and others; and now in the times of the Gospel, the same Spirit still animates God's children, and inclines their hearts still to seek the good of Jerusalem; how do the apostles in several epistles testify this disposition in them? "God is my witness whom I serve with my spirit in the Gospel of his Son, that without ceasing I make mention of you (says that apostle to the Church of Rome) always in my prayers," (Romans 1:9); so, "making mention of you in my prayers, that the God of our Lord Jesus Christ, the Father of glory, may give unto you," (Ephesians 1:16-17).

Yes, so much religion have the saints of God before us placed in this duty of praying for Jerusalem, that they have deprecated the neglect of this as a most abominable sin, "As for me, God forbid that I should sin against you, in ceasing to pray for you." (1 Samuel 12:23); no, have imprecated a curse on themselves, if ever they should be so wretched, "If I forget thee O Jerusalem, let my right hand forget her cunning. If I do not remember thee, let my tongue cleave to the roof of my mouth, if I prefer not Jerusalem above my chief joy," (Psalm 135:5-6); it is one of the greatest judgments that can befall a prophet, to be silenced. Witness Zachariah whose unbelief God punished with this, as an only judgment; witness those amongst ourselves, that have had their mouths stopped by the violent hand of man, who know what it is to have the word of God as a fire in their bones, and no vent for it; yet even to this, the Prophet here curses himself, "If I forget thee O Jerusalem," if I do not remember to mourn for you, let my tongue cleave to the roof of my mouth; the good Lord be merciful to every one of us, and pardon all our forgetfulness of Jerusalem, whom we have as much cause and reason to remember as ever any had.

Is not Jerusalem the city of God, the house of God, the peculiar of God, the delight of God, the crown of glory, the royal diadem in the hand of God? Is it not the love, the dove, the spouse, the sister, the body, the fullness, the glory of Jesus Christ? (Hebrews 12:22, 1 Timothy 3:15, Psalm 35:4, Titus 2:14, Isaiah 62:4, Isaiah 62:2, Song of Solomon 5:2, Ephesians 1:23, 2 Corinthians 8:23). And in all these respects, does it not deserve our prayers?

2. And secondly, are not earth and hell up in arms against Jerusalem? Are not men and devils in league together, to confound and destroy Jerusalem, the church? "They have taken craft counsel against thy people, and consulted against thy hidden ones. They have said, come, and let us cut them off from being a nation. That the name of Israel may be no more in

remembrance. Gebal, Ammon, and Amalek," (Psalm 83:3-4). And does Jerusalem not in this respect now need our prayers?

3. And thirdly, has the Lord not made promises to Jerusalem of these things we are to pray for? Of truth and peace, "I will cure them, and reveal abundance of truth and peace to them," (Jeremiah 33:6). As also, of praise, "It shall be to me a name of joy, a praise and an honor before all the nations of the earth," (verse 9) and, "I will make you a name and a praise among the people of the earth," (Zephaniah 3:20). And is the Lord not able to accomplish these promises notwithstanding all their counter-machinations of his enemies? "My counsel shall stand, and I will do all my pleasure," (Isaiah 46:10).

4. Yet fourthly, it is not the Lord's pleasure to accomplish these things unto his Church but in and by his people's prayers, "(Call unto me and I will answer thee, and shew thee great and mighty things which thou knowest not," (Jeremiah 33:3), "I will yet for this be enquired of by the house of Israel to do it for them," (Ezekiel 36:37).

Sed quo ferori? Some use I would gladly make of this point, if I knew what; I might afford variety of profitable instructions, but it is not for me to presume to instruct so honorable, learned, and religious an assembly; give me leave to apologize for myself with Elihu, "I said I am of few days, and ye are old, wherefore I was afraid and durst not shew you mine opinion; I said days should speak, and multitudes of years should teach wisdom," (Job 32:6). The Lord knows, glad would I have been to sit at any of your feet to learn, rather than to stand here to teach, and to receive rather than to give instruction, therefore I decline that work.

In the next place, this truth might serve for reproof, and if such an application would not lead me besides my authority, O with what vehemence might a man from here, in the name and by the Spirit of our Lord Jesus Christ thunder indignation and wrath on the heads of those who though they have usurped and possessed the place of such as should be the Lord's remembrancers, yet instead of performing the duty of this text have practiced the clean contrary, instead of praying that God would establish his Church in truth, have endeavored nothing but to undermine the truth, to subvert, adulterate the truth; "their folly (as the Apostle speaks) is manifest unto all men,"(2 Timothy 3:9), God has unmasked them, and all that will see may see their design was to let in such an inundation of popery and socinianism, as should have drowned the truth of God forever. Instead of praying that God would establish his Church in peace, they have acted the part of those unclean spirits, the frogs spoken of, stirring up the kings of the earth to battle against the Church of God, (Revelation 16:14); first in Scotland, who were incendiaries, what was the fuel of the war there? And since that in England, have the wars of both kingdoms not had the same fuel and fomenters? And who are they but the Jesuit clergy of England, who like the unclean spirit we read of in Mark 9, fearing they shall now be cast out of their long possession, rent and tear the kingdom and lay it wallowing (not as he did the child there, in its foam, but) in its blood? What shall I speak of such a clergy? Who instead of praying that God would make his Church a praise, have endeavored nothing more than to rob the Church of all that might make it praiseworthy, instead of desiring that the Church might enjoy fullness of ordinances, endeavoring to strip the Church of them all; to abolish Sabbaths, to bring the delight of days, the Queen of days under the curse of Job's birth day, "Let it not be joined to the days of the year, let it not come into the number of the months; to excommunicate preaching and praying," and cast them quite out of the Church; to turn the sacrament of the Lord's Supper unto a sacrifice on the altar; Instead of praying that all ordinances and offices might be administered according to Christ's rule and order, would have all things in God's house and worship done according to their own fancy, will, lust, and humor. What shall we say to such a clergy? (they dote on the name still, let them enjoy it). Aristotle speaks of a little worm that is pestilently noxious and destructive to beehives; no less noxious and destructive as our enemies, the greatest part of them being to the true Church of

God among us; against whom the Church of God may power out as sad complaints to her Lord Jesus Christ, as sometimes she did, "The watchmen, the keepers of the wall, found me, they smote me, they took away my veil," (Song of Solomon 5). Let such read their doom, "their judgment now of a long time lingereth not, and their damnation sleepeth not," (2 Peter 2).

I had not turned aside to this reproof, (for I look for none of this generation here this day) had it not been to provoke myself and you to a more serious and deep humiliation for those abominations of the late times, which though many of us have seen and observed even then, and some of us have felt and smarted under its violences, yet few I fear among us have had our hearts so humbled for their iniquity, as they should have been. The Lord help us so to take to heart this day, our own and other men's sins, that he may forgive our iniquities, and heal our land.

But I return to my main point for you the hearers, and the only boldness I assume, brethren and fathers, is but to do as much as Naaman's servant did to his Lord, exhort you to do that which you know God would have you do, pray for Jerusalem. And I am confident I might spare even this; it is our work daily; but God having called me this day to speak unto you, for Zion's sake I cannot hold my peace; *Qui monet ut facias quod facis, dum monet laudat (And he warns that you do what you do, as long as he warns with priases).*

Is it the duty of ministers in a special manner to pray incessantly that God would establish Jerusalem and make it a praise in the earth? Then let every one of us by solemn engagements to God and to his Church bind ourselves to the performance of this duty. And surely brethren if ever there were times that called for this duty, if ever there were men called to this duty, this is the time, we are the men.

First, for the time; if ever there were a time that commanded the most importune and incessant prayers of all God's ministers and people (for here I will take in all) that they should cry mightily to the Lord night and day in the behalf of Jerusalem, "keep no silence, give him no rest, till he establish and make Jerusalem a praise in the earth," if ever there were a time that exacted this, now is the time. Had I art or grace enough to present before you the lively (or rather) ghastly, deadly face of Jerusalem, the Churches of Christ Jesus at this time, I know it would command tears and prayers from the most flinty heart in this congregation. Could I let you see Jerusalem like that man in the parable that went down from, "Jerusalem, fallen among thieves, and by them stripped and wounded and left half dead," (Luke 10:30), while many, too many with the priests and Levites passing by on the other side of the way, and will not see (though they cannot but see) the Church's bleeding miseries, "amongst all her lovers there is none to comfort her," (Lamentations 1:2). "Zion spreadeth

forth her hands, and there is none to comfort her,"
(Lamentations 1:17). Zion spreads forth her hands from sea to
sea, from one nation to another people, and there is none to
comfort her, "there is none to guide her amongst all the sons
whom she hath brought forth, neither is there any that takes
her by the hand of all the sons that she has brought up,"
(Isaiah 51:18). O were I able to express this to your life, you
would say, if ever there were a time for you to show yourselves
as the good Samaritan to bestow, as he did, your wine, your
oil, your money, nay your tears, your prayers, your blood on
the healing of the Church's wounds, now is the time.

Or could I let you see the Church of Jerusalem, as John
saw her in that Revelation, which was given to him by Christ
Jesus, in the same condition, though not in the same clothing;
a, "woman clothed, not (as there) with the sun, but with a
cloud, not having moon nor sun under her feet, but a globe of
flames, a field of blood under her feet, not as there with a
crown of twelve stars on her head, but rather in Tamar's dress
and posture, (2 Samuel 13:19), who with ashes on her head,
and her garment of diverse colors (the ensign of her virginity
and royalty) rent and torn, and with her hands on her head
going forth crying, such may we conceive the dress and
posture of the Church of Christ to be, she now, as there,
"cryeth travailing and pained to be delivered," (Revelation 12);
in this pained condition the Church has been now almost

these three years, ever since the beginning of this parliament, the Church of God amongst us has been in travail, crying and pained to be delivered; and all this while, as there, the great red dragon stands before the woman to devour the child as soon as it is born. O, the sight of the Church in such a sad condition might force a tear from a stone, a prayer from a speechless, heartless man; but from ministers, from those that are the Lord's remembrancers, methinks it might draw tears enough to rinse the earth from blood, and prayers enough to offer violence to heaven.

But not to speak parabolically, but plainly, I say again, if ever there were a time that commanded the most importune and incessant prayers of all God's ministers and people, now is the time; was there ever a time in which the Church of God was more shaken, more in danger to have both her pillars of truth and peace broken, reduced to dust, to nothing, than at this time? The enemies of the Church have a long time sought to undermine the truth, but now, they raise arms against the truth, they plant open battery against the truth. And for our peace, where is it? *Terras reliquit (the lands have been left)*, it has taken to itself the wings of a dove, and forsaking the earth has fled to heaven, frightened here with the sound of the trumpet, the alarm of war, and the cry of blood. We may chronicle of our age, that which the prophet Azariah spoke of some ages of Israel, "In those times there was no peace to him that went out, nor to him that came in, but great vexations were on all the inhabitants of the countries. And nation was destroyed of nation, and city of city. For God did vex them with all adversity," (2 Chronicles 15:5-6). Never was this poor Church and people in a more broken, distressed condition in regard of peace civil, nor scarcely ever worse in regard of peace ecclesiastical. Now when there are so many swords in England and in Ireland drawn against the protestants; O that we should be even at daggers drawing one against another! O the bitter divisions and digladiations of protestants among themselves in these bleeding times!, "For the divisions of Reuben there are great searchings of heart." Holy Ridley and Hooper, though in the times of the peace and liberty of the Gospel, they could never agree about black and white, but had many wrathful bickerings, yet in time of persecution for the Gospel, they could, as their own expression is, agree in red; when God came to put them together in tears, and sufferings, and blood, they could forget all differences of judgment then, and love and live and die together as brethren. Do those know what spirit they are of, that at such a time as this, when all the true-hearted protestants in England are put in one calamitous, suffering, bleeding, condition, are yet quarreling about their own opinions, weakening the protestant party by subdivisions, which if united is scarcely enough to withstand the common adversary; should this be if we had not lost our peace with God? As the Holy Spirit speaks of the calamities of the Church in Judah, (2 Kings 24:3), so may we say of the calamities on the Church of England, "Surely at the commandment of the Lord came this on England;" and the Lord grant that the following words are not verified in their time, the Lord grant this to not be come on us, to remove England out of his sight. But however we may take up the Church's lamentation, "Thou hast removed me far from peace; aye, and as far from praise the crown is fallen from our head," (Lamentations 3:17, 5:16), we have become a reproach to our neighbors, a scorn, a derision, a byword, a shaking of the head; those few of us that adhere to the protestant religion and cause, are represented to the world at home and abroad, as sectaries, Anabaptists, rebels, that if ever there were a time for us to cry to God to scatter those clouds of blood, confusion, and contempt that cover the face of the Church, to bring forth our judgment as the light; and our righteousness as the morning, now is the time, "Ye that are the Lord's remembrancers, keep no silence, give him no rest, till he establish, and till he make Jerusalem a praise in the earth."

And if ever men were called to this work, we are called to it; as ministers; as ministers selected from the rest of our brethren, to this present service, whereunto we desire to sanctify ourselves this day. As ministers it does *ex officio* (from our office) belong to us, to be the Lord's remembrancers. To put the Lord in mind of Jerusalem; you know what order the Lord took, that the priests, the ministers of the Lord, under the law, might continually remember Israel, the Church of God unto the Lord, the high priest was to bear the names of the twelve tribes on his shoulders, engraved on twelve stones: "that he might bear them on his heart for a memorial before the Lord continually," (Exodus 28:12,29); they were to be the priest's remembrancers, that he should be the Lord's remembrance, to put the priest in mind of putting God in mind of Israel, by praying for them. This type is properly applicable to Christ, who is the only High Priest of his Church, yet so far as the ministers of the Gospel are Christ's substitutes on earth, so far this may (at least by way of allusion) be applied to them, for so far there ought to be in them the same disposition toward Jerusalem that was in Christ Jesus, that as Christ wept over Jerusalem, so should they; as he remembered Jerusalem, so should they; he by way of meritorious intercession, they by way of ministerial intercession, to bear Jerusalem on their shoulders and on their hearts continually, whenever they address themselves into God's presence, (1 Timothy 2:1). Jerusalem is engraved on the hand of God, and therefore should be engraved on the hearts of his ministers, and is, if God has laid his hand on their hearts. You know the story of that heathen priest that began to offer sacrifice before a battle writ Victoria (or some such like word) in the palm of his hand, and in emboweling the sacrifice laid his hand on the heart of the beast, and left the characters of the same word there, that what had been written on the hand of the priest was read on the heart of the sacrifice, "Behold I have graven thee, saith God to Jerusalem, on the palms of my hands," (Isaiah 49:16), and look how many hearts there are of Nobles, or Gentry, or Ministers, or others, on whom God has laid his hand, I do not doubt that the same configuration on them is engraved on the hand of God. That as God himself cannot forget Jerusalem, because it is engraven on their hearts; that as Queen Mary said of Callice, when I am dead, rip me and you shall find Callice at my heart. So there is a many a godly man, and many a godly minister especially who might say, when I am dead, rip me and you shall find Jerusalem at my heart, "That sacred name is deeply engraven there; If I forget thee O Jerusalem, let my right hand forget her cunning." All you that are the Lord's remembrancers, you that have Jerusalem written in your hearts, keep no silence, give him no rest, till he establish, and till he make Jerusalem a praise in the earth. If ever a man were called to this work, ministers are.

And if ever ministers were called to this work, the more especially are you whom it has pleased God by the authority of the honorable houses of Parliament to call together to debate and advise of such things as may be necessary, or conducing to the establishment of truth, peace, and beauty in the Churches of Christ Jesus; and does it not then especially lie on you to keep no silence, give the Lord no rest, *till he establish, etc.* I say *till he establish,* for, except the Lord build the house, they labor in vain that build it; *except the Lord reform the Church, it is to no purpose to go about to reform it*; except the Lord set up the pillars of peace and truth in his Church, it is labor lost to endeavor it; You that are called to this great work, you of all men ought to keep no silence, give the Lord no rest, till he establish, and till he make Jerusalem a praise in the earth.

I do not need to tell you how many eyes and expectations there are on this assembly, I do not speak it as a matter of boasting, but as a matter of trembling and lying low before the Lord this day, from all the parts of the kingdom, from all the parts of the Christian world, the eyes of all the people of God are on you; foreign Churches have their eyes towards you, waiting to see what you will advise for the more utter extinction of popery, and effecting of a more near and full union between us and the rest of the reformed Churches; all the parts of the kingdoms have their faces and voices towards you, I think I hear a voice from all the corners of the land coming up to this assembly, to be by you reported to the honorable houses of Parliament; a voice like that of the poor woman to the King on the wall, "help, help," for the Lord's sake, "help." "Help us" to better ministers, help us to better ordinances, help us to purer worship, help us to better discipline, help us to remove those things that deter us from the Lord's table, help our tender consciences to more liberty, *etc.* I know it brethren, God's people, most of them look for help by this assembly, through your faithful advice given to the honorable houses of Parliament. And may you not answer as he did there, "except the Lord help thee, where should I help thee?" there is such an *Augea Stabulum* of corruption and confusion in doctrine, discipline, worship, in all; that (verily) unless that God who is able, "to remove the iniquity of the land in one day, and to cause the prophet and unclean spirit to pass out of the land," (Zechariah 3:9,13:2), unless that great God set his hand to this great work, it will never prosper; and yet if it should not prosper, the sin would be laid at your door, and you would bear the reproach of it to all memory; therefore great need to importune God to come down and own his work, "O that thou wouldest rent the heavens and come down, that the mountains might flow at thy presence!" You among all the rest of the Lord's remembrancers, keep no silence, give him no rest, *till he establish, and till he make Jerusalem a praise in the earth.*

And one more thing, what I know you have all taught others yourselves, now put in practice, pursue your prayers, with your endeavors; what you pray for, contend for. As you pray that God would establish his Church in truth, so with united endeavors labor to raise up and establish the decayed truth among us, vindicating the truths of the protestant religion from all popish, Arminian, Socinian, Anabaptist, Antinomian, and all other *errors* whatsoever. And as you pray that God would establish his Church in peace, so labor to work out the Church's peace with God, by endeavoring a removal of all pollutions, or profaneness no matter what they are, those which have turned God into an enemy to us. And then labor the Church's peace with its own members; which certainly you shall establish, if denying yourselves and laying by all pre-engagements to your own opinions, desires, ways, you shall willingly and unanimously consent to that which on just and pious debate shall be found to be the way and truth of God; which I do not doubt but through his grace you shall all do. Believe it brethren, in your union will be laid a happy foundation of union through the whole kingdom; if you agree in this assembly, I dare think to promise myself, and you, a happy agreement amongst all that fear God in the nation. And then we need take no thought for the third thing, peace with our enemies. God will either subdue them under us, or make them be at peace with us. Only let neither the desire of peace with them, nor peace among ourselves, bribe us to tolerate anything in the Church of God that might make him to be at war with us.

And lastly, as you pray that God would make the Church *a praise*, so endeavor that also; endeavoring that the Church of Christ may enjoy all those liberties and ordinances that are purchased for her by the blood and bequeathed to her in the testament of her Lord Jesus. That all her ways may be ordered according to the rule of God's Word. That the Gospel may run and be glorified. That those two great illuminating ordinances of preaching and catechizing, which are as the greater and lesser lights of heaven, may have such liberty, encouragement, maintenance, that all the earth may be filled with the knowledge of the Lord, (Romans 15:5-6). This do, and prosper. And that you may so do this, the God of patience and consolation grant you to be like-minded one towards another, according to Christ Jesus, that you may with one mind and one mouth glorify God, even the Father of our Lord Jesus Christ. *Amen, Amen.*

A FUNERAL SERMON

A sermon preached at the funerals of the Reverent and faithful servant of Jesus Christ in the work of the Gospel, Mr. Samuel Collins, Pastor of the Church of Christ at Braintree in Essex.

Who exchanged this life for immortality In the 77th year of his age, in the 46th year of his ministry there, in the year of our Lord, 1657.

Preached by Matthew Newcomen, Minister of the Gospel in the Church of Dedham. (London. Printed by D. Maxwell for W. Weekley at Ipswich, and are to be sold by J. Rothwel at the Fountain in Cheapside, and Rich. Tomlins at the Sun and Bible in Pye-corner. 1658.)

THE SERMON

Acts 13:36, "For David after he had served his own generation by the will of God fell on sleep, and was laid to be with his fathers, and saw corruption."

Funeral sermons are condemned much by some in these times; and funeral speeches, speeches in commendation of the deceased much more, yet certainly there is a warrantable use of both, though the latter of these has suffered much abuse. Might the *Practice of Antiquity*, and the *Custom of the Church* (which in things not precisely determined in Scripture with the Apostle Paul are no contemptible arguments:) might these, I say, be heard, the controversy would soon be ended, (1 Corinthians 11:19). For it has been the practice of the Church of Christ *ab antique* to solemnize the funerals, especially of such as have been eminent in their lives, with such kind of speeches or sermons, as appears in the writings of many, the most illustrious lights, especially of the eastern Churches.

And for warrant from Scripture, we have this much to *say*:

First, for the people of God, when one of their brethren or sisters is taken from them by the stroke of death, to assemble themselves together to give him a solemn and honorable interment. This is undoubtedly and beyond all question warranted from the frequent (I might say almost constant) practice of the saints in the Old Testament and in the New. Instances in the Old Testament, you have in the burial of Jacob, and Aaron, and Samuel, and others, whom I spare to mention, for they are so numerous.

I shall only mention one in the New Testament in the Gospel Church, and that is the instance of Steven, "Devout men carried Steven to his burial, and made great lamentation over him," (Acts 8:2). Though then it was a dangerous time *flagrante persecution*, the fire of persecution being newly broken forth on the Christian Church, and Steven being the man that had been sacrificed in those flames as the first fruits of the Gospel, yet they were not, they would not be discouraged from this work of humanity and Christian charity, but devout men carried Steven to his burial.

Devout men. It is likely that there were more of them than would just serve to carry his corpse to the grave. If there were some that had so much zeal and charity, and courage in them, as to carry him, questionless, there were others that had so much zeal, charity, and courage as to attend him: "Devout men carried Steven to the grave, and made great lamentation over him." It is not then unbecoming of devout, godly men, to accompany the corpse of a deceased friend, brother, fellow

Christian to the grave, nor to take up a lamentation over him, and say as the prophet of Bethel over his fellow prophet, "Alas my brother," (1 Kings 13:30), or, "Ah brother, ah sister, ah Lord, or ah his glory," (Jeremiah 22:18). This is clearly warranted, you see by precedents from Scripture.

This being warranted by precedent from Scripture, I assume in the second place, it cannot be unwarrantable for a minister of the Gospel, when a company of Christians are thus met together to attend a burial, to take that opportunity of speaking to them from God and from his Word something that may be seasonable and suiting to the present providence; something that may put them in remembrance of their own mortality, and quicken them to prepare for death, to improve the time of the present life, or to lay hold on eternal life, etc. (Some or all of which are the ordinary subjects and the proper scopes of our funeral sermons) for a minister in this way to do, cannot justly be thought unwarrantable. Certainly that charge, that solemn charge which the Apostle gave Timothy and in him all the ministers of the Gospel, "To preach the Word, to be instant in season and out of season," (2 Timothy 4:2), does more than warrant this. When is a sermon of mortality in season, if not at a funeral when an example of mortality, *ocules ferire*, lies before our eyes? When is an exhortation to prepare ourselves for death seasonable, if not at a funeral, when a real spectacle of the spoil and triumph of death is before our eyes? When is a sermon to excite us to make sure of eternal life more in season than at a funeral, where we see by ocular and evident experience how short, how vanishing, how uncertain this present life is? But why should I stand discoursing any longer about this particular, when God himself has witnessed from heaven his approbation of funeral sermons by blessing them to the good of souls, as some of you, I hope, can witness from your own experience. And not many days have passed since I heard a Reverent and very successful minister of the Gospel say,[11] "That he had seen the greatest fruit of funeral sermons of all the sermons that ever he preached."

Thirdly, funeral speeches, though I have not used them much, nor shall, yet I dare not condemn those who do use them, so long as it is done with moderation, and with caution, and where there is indeed just cause of commendation. For why may I not make a speech in the praise of one deceased, as well as another write a poem in the praise of one deceased? Why may I not by mentioning the virtues and graces, the usefulness and serviceableness of a deceased Christian, labor to affect my own heart and the hearts of others either with thankfulness to God for the graces bestowed on him, or with grief for our loss in the withdrawing of him?

---

[11] My reverent friend and neighbor Mr. John Wall, preacher at Michaels Cornhill.

2. With holy emulation to imitate and follow his example and patter. Why may I not do this in a speech, as well as another in a poem? And I am sure this latter has precedent in Scripture; thus Jeremy lamented for Josiah and made poems, verses in memorial of him for the people to sing, as you may read, (2 Chronicles 35:25).

Objection. But you will say, Josiah, there was not a man like him. Well, it may be so; what do you then say of Saul and Jonathan? David, you know, wrote a poem in the praise of them, "The beauty of Israel is fallen on the high places. How are the mighty fallen?" (2 Samuel 1). What shall we say of that poem of David? Was it a flash of wit, a pang of natural affection? God forbid that we should think so. Was he not rather guided by the same blessed and Holy Spirit that inspired him in his other poems? Surely yes; or this would never have been legitimated and canonized in Scripture amongst the rest. From where I infer, that it is lawful and agreeable to the will of God, and the wisdom of his Spirit, to make an honorable mention of such when they are dead, who have done things *worthy of praise* when they lived.

So much for the justifying of our solemn meeting and action on this occasion. I now come to the text. In this chapter from the 16th verse to the 41st, you have an excellent sermon preached by Paul (not the first sermon that Paul ever preached, but) the first sermon of Paul's that the Holy Spirit put on record. Preached at Antioch in Pisidia (so called to distinguish it from that other Antioch which was in Syria) where the name of Christian was first minted, and the disciples were first baptized into the Christian name, (Acts 11:26) from which Antioch it was that Paul was separated, (Acts 13:1) and sent forth to this journey, in which journey coming first to Selucia, (verse 4) and from there sailing to Cyprus (verse 4) after some time there spent in preaching the Gospel, they came to Perga in Pamphilia, (verse 13) and from there to Antioch in Pisidia, (verse 14).

To this city Paul and Barnabas (guided by the Spirit of God) came and went (the text says), "into the synagogue on the Sabbath day, and sat down." The synagogue was the place where the people of the Jews ordinarily met together every Sabbath day for the reading of Moses and the Prophets, and the performing of other duties of worship unto God. Here Paul and Barnabas resort, and here they sat down as quietly and composedly as any other that were present in the assembly, offering no interruption nor disturbance all the while the Scriptures were in reading.

"And after the reading of the law and of the prophets, the rulers of the synagogues sent unto them, saying, Ye men and brethren, if you have any word of exhortation for the people, say on," (verse 13). The Evangelist Luke here shows (Calvin says) *Non omnibus permissum fuisse loqui.* It was not free for anyone that would to speak in that assembly, but that the work of exhorting lay on certain men, even those whom the evangelist calls the rulers of the synagogue, it belonged to them after the reading of Moses and the Prophets, to instruct and exhort the people out of that which had been read. Therefore, Paul and Barnabas do not presently as soon as the exercise of reading was finished fall *a' speaking*, lest by their overmuch hastiness they should cause disturbance, *sed modeste expectant*, but modestly expect till they have leave given them to speak; and that by those, *penes quos public consensus autoritas erat*, to whom authority in the synagogue belonged by public consent the rulers of the synagogue, and they supposing Paul and Barnabas, even by their countenance and garb, *Nonesse vulgares homines* (as one speaks) to be no ordinary men, sent to them saying, "Men and brethren, if you have any word of exhortation for the people, say on."

We know, Calvin says, how corrupt the state of the people of the Jews was at this time, and the Evangelist tells us afterwards in the process of history, how proud and refractory these very Jews of Antioch were in rejecting the grace of Christ. Yet thus much good, says he, remained still among them, that there was decency and order in their assemblies. *Quo magis pudenda est deformis confusio qua hodie inter eos qui Christiani haberi volunt conspicitur.* By so much the more shameful, he says, is that deformed confusion that is seen at this time among those that would be counted Christians. Gualter also takes notice of several things commendable and imitable in this Jewish assembly, as their coming together on the Sabbath day, their demeaning themselves decently and modestly in their assembly, their reading of Moses and the Prophets, and in conclusion, *Et illud quoque Laudem meretur (And it also deserves praise)*. And this also is praise worthy (he says) that no man among them takes liberty to speak, unless he is lawfully required; therefore Paul and Barnabas, though sent by the Holy Spirit, would not speak till called to it; *Minime itaque ferenda est Anabaptistarum intemperies, So little is needed by the Baptists in temperature.*

Being thus invited, "Paul stood up, and beckoning with his hand," (verse 16) (as men do that would bespeak silence and attention in those to whom they speak) he said as follows: (verse 41).

In which speech of Paul's, we have considerable, first, the introduction that Paul uses to his speech, (verse 13). Secondly, the narration, or body of the speech in the following verses.

First, the introduction, in these words, "Men of Israel, and ye that fear God, give audience." Where, mark the loving and respective compellations that Paul uses, "Men of Israel, and ye that fear God!" How does Paul (being a stranger) know that there were any among them that feared God? They even showed afterwards that they were so far from fearing God, as they, "blasphemed him," (verse 45). But that was more than Paul knew. At the present Paul found them meeting together in the worship of God, as men should do that fear God, and therefore he hoped and judged the best of them, "Men and brethren, and all ye that fear God, hearken."

Having thus prefaced, he proceeds to his discourse, which discourse or sermon of Paul's may, as one says, be well called, "A short sum or epitome of the whole Scripture." But especially, it is a history of the manifold grace and mercy of God towards his Church and people.

First, in their election, the, "God of this people of Israel chose our fathers," (verse 17). Secondly, in his magnifying them in Egypt, by the wonders which he there wrought for them, "And exalted the people when they dwelt as strangers in the land of Egypt." Thirdly, in his bringing them out of there, "And brought them out of it with an high hand," (verse 17). Fourthly, in his indulgence and patience towards them in the wilderness, "And above the time of forty years suffered he their manners in the wilderness," (verse 18). Fifthly, in putting them into possession of the land of Canaan, "And when he had destroyed seven nations in the land of Canaan, he divided their land to them by lot," (verse 19). Sixthly, in establishing a civil government among them, first by Judges, "He gave unto them Judges," (verse 20). And afterwards (upon their desire) by Kings, delivering that government, first to Saul, "Afterward they desired a King, and God gave unto them Saul," (verse 21). But the kingly government was established by God on the house of David, "He raised up unto them David to be their King," (verse 22) and having recited these particular mercies of God to his people, he makes a great leap from the days of David to the days of the Messiah, the Son of David, and shuts up his catalogue of mercies with the mention of the greatest and freshest mercy, namely God's sending a Savior out of David's loins according to his promise, "Of this man's seed hath God according to his promise raised unto Israel a Savior Jesus," (verse 23).

Now this, being the principal nail that the Apostle had to drive and fasten in that assembly, he spends the rest of his sermon in driving that nail home; proving that this promise made to David was fulfilled in the same Jesus, whom their rulers at Jerusalem crucified. And this he proves, first, by John's coming, as his forerunner, to preach repentance according to the prophecies of Isaiah and Malachi, "When John had first preached before his coming at the baptism of repentance to all the people of Israel," (Isaiah 40:3, Malachi 3:1, 4:5-6). Secondly, he proves it by the express testimony that John gave of him, he said, "I am not he, but behold there cometh one after me," (verse 25). Thirdly, he proves it by the fulfilling of the ancient prophecies of Scripture in his cruel and causeless death, "For they that dwelt at Jerusalem and their rulers, because they knew him not, nor yet the voice of the Prophets which are read every Sabbath day, they have fulfilled them in condemning him. And though they found no cause of death in him, yet they delivered him to Pilate that he should be slain," (verse 27-28). Fourthly, he proves the same thing by his resurrection from the dead, "And when they had fulfilled all that was written of him, they took him down from the tree and laid him in the sepulcher; But God raised him from the dead," (verse 29:30). Which resurrection the Lord Jesus is *proved,*

1. By the testimony of eye-witnesses, "And he was seen many days of them who came up with him from Galilee to Jerusalem, who are his witnesses to the people," (verse 31).

2. He proves this resurrection of Christ by testimonies of Scripture foretelling his resurrection, (verse 34-37). Then you have the application of all this to the hearers in particular, (verse 38-39). And so the Apostle concludes his sermon with a serious admonition to his hearers not to despise nor reject this offered grace.

In all, which discourse and carriage of Paul, you have nothing but what really evidences that blessed and Holy Spirit, whose fruits are, "Love, peace, long-suffering, gentleness, goodness, faith, meekness, temperance," (Galatians 5:22-23). Here is not one bitter boisterous intemperate word in all this discourse of Paul's.

How far are they from this apostolic Spirit, that pretend in these times to be the only apostolic men, and to be guided and acted by as infallible a Spirit, as the Apostles themselves were. They will tell you, the Spirit moves them, and bids them, "go to such a town, to such a meeting place." Well, what do they do when they are there? Do they sit as Paul and Barnabas did, and demean themselves with gravity and reverence becoming such an assembly? No, but carry themselves in such a proud, scornful, wild, disdainful manner, that their very presence is a disturbance to the whole congregation. Do they wait until they are invited and called to speak, as Paul and Barnabas did? No, but soon as the last word is out of the minister's mouth (if not before) they blow their trumpet, sound their alarm, bid defiance to him, his doctrine and calling.

And when they speak, what? Do they use sober, meek, and gentle speeches, as the Apostle Paul here, "Men of Israel, and all ye that fear God." Do they bring clear evidence, Scripture arguments, and solid reasons, as the Apostle Paul here does? No, but they break out into bitterest railings and cursings, condemning for hypocrites, and damned, and full of the devil all but themselves. Whether these men are acted by an apostolic Spirit or by a diabolical spirit, whether their tongues are touched with a coal from the Lord's altar or set on fire of hell, it is easy to judge, if it is true what our Savior says, "By thy words thou shalt be justified, and by thy words thou shalt be condemned," (Matthew 12:37).

Out of this whole discourse of Paul's I have made choice of the words of the 36th verse to insist on at this time, and on this occasion, "But David after he had served his generation, by the will of God fell on sleep, and was laid unto his fathers, and saw corruption."

Which words are a prevention of an objection that might be made against a Scripture which the Apostle in the verse immediately foregoing had cited out of the sixteenth Psalm to prove the resurrection of Christ, in these words, "Thou shalt not suffer thine holy one to see corruption." Now, lest the Jews should in their hearts object that this place might be spoken of David himself, the Apostle anticipates this, and shows that this place cannot be competent to David properly and directly, but only as he was a type of Christ, and by way of participation, as he should, together with the rest of the godly, be raised up by Christ, "For David, after he had served his own generation by the will of God, fell on sleep, and was laid to his fathers, and saw corruption."

In these words we have considerable points. First, the person spoken of, David; secondly, the employment of this person, he served; thirdly, the object on which he bestowed his pains and service, his own generation; fourthly, the moving or ordering, or regulating cause of this, the will of God; fifthly, the issue and event of this in three particulars, first, he fell on sleep, secondly, he was laid to his fathers, thirdly, he saw corruption.

David, a man whom God found out and framed according to his own heart, and took from following *the ewes great with young* to feed and rule his people Israel, whom God advanced from a mean and low condition to the highest pinnacle of honor, setting his throne higher than the kings of the earth. (Psalm 89:29).

He served, not himself, by an exorbitant, arbitrary government, as his predecessor Saul had done, but he served others, he served all, he served his own generation.

That word, generation, is a word of frequent and various use in Scripture. I shall not lead you through them all, I shall only give you notice of four or five.

First, sometimes it signifies a succession of men begetting and propagating one another, so in the first of Matthew there are reckoned from Abraham to Christ forty-two generations, that is, successions of children standing up in their father's rooms.

Secondly, sometimes it signifies all the men that live together at the same time; so it is said of Noah, "That he was a just man and perfect in his generations," (Genesis 6:9), that is, among the man of that age in which he lived.

Thirdly, it signifies men of a like quality and disposition, though they live in several ages and periods of time, as, "God is in the generation of the righteous," (Psalm 14:5) and, "This is the generation of them that seek thee," (Psalm 24:6).

Fourthly, sometimes it signifies a family or nation; So, "Verily, I say unto you, this generation shall not pass till all these things be fulfilled," (Matthew 24:34). Which words cannot be understood of that particular race of the Jews which were living on the earth in our Savior's days, for they are passed away long ago, but must be understood of the people and nation of the Jews in all their decurrent successions. And the meaning of the words must be this, that whatever devastations and desolations should come on Jerusalem according to the predictions of that chapter, the Jews should yet remain a people, a nation distinct from all other nations, though scattered among them all the world over, even to the coming of Christ in judgment. That where other nations living among strangers become incorporate with them in a few generations, only the Jews wherever they live still remain a nation distinct from all other nations. And this is the sense of the word generation in that place. So in this place it is to be taken in the second sense, "David served his generation," that is, that company of men with whom he was contemporary, who lived all the same time that he himself lived. Unless you will add a fifth sense of the word, by which it signifies the age or term of life, which sense some contend for in that fore-mentioned place, (Matthew 24:34) and so the meaning is, "David served his own generation," that is, David was a useful, serviceable man all the days of his life, even to his dying day, for, "David after he had served his own generation by the will of God, fell on sleep."

By the *will of God*, or by the *counsel of God*, which *Incisum* or branch of the verse is variously pointed in several copies; some cut it off from the foregoing words and affix it to the word following, and make a comma at the foregoing Greek word, they read it this way, "By the will of God he fell on sleep." So Arias Montauus in his interlineary. And so some other copies; and this punctuation Erasmus followed in his Latin translation. But Beza rejects this pointing wholly, and says *Haec distincio neque in vetustis codicibus reperitur,neque ulla ratione nititur*. Neither does Stephanas take any notice of it in his *Varia Lectiones* on the New Testament. Therefore, the more true and right reading of the text seems to be that which our translation follows, in which that phrase, "By the will of God" is annexed to thee words foregoing, and the text so reads, "For

David after he had served his own generation by the will of God, fell on sleep."

And yet even so read, the words as Camerarius has observed, have *quandum*, a kind of ambiguity, although so far from being hurtful that it is profitable for that phrase, "By the will of God," may be referred either to the generation, and so the meaning is, David served that generation which it was the will and counsel of God to cast on him; or else it may be referred to the service that David did to his generation, and so the meaning is, David served his own generation, not after his own will, or fancy, or humor, or the humors, fancies, or wills of other men, but after the will of God, "For David after he had served his generation by the will of God, fell on sleep."

Fell on sleep. That is a phrase often used in Scripture to signify death, especially of the righteous, it is usually said of them, as of David here, "he fell on sleep."

And was laid to his fathers. That phrase if often used in Scripture of the burial and interment of the saints, "he was laid to his fathers."

And saw corruption. That is, his body rotted in the grave. *Videre significant sentire aut experiri aliquid.*

The words (like Joseph) are a fruitful branch, from where might be gathered many comfortable and profitable doctrines, as *namely,*

First, in the general from, the mention which the Holy Spirit here makes of David, which you see here as in other places of Scripture is altogether honorable, here is no mention of any disservice David did in his generation. Not one word of his being the occasion of the death of 85 of the Lord's priests in one day, they, their wives and their children; not a word of his defiling Bathsheba or murdering Uriah, or the numbering of the people which cost the lives of seventy thousand in three days. Not a word of any of this, but only what a useful, serviceable man he was.

There observe in the first place, that God values those that are in Christ, and have repented of their sins, not according to the evil, but the good that has been in them.

Secondly, and more particularly, that several particular persons have their several particular generations to serve in. David here in the text served his generation, so Noah did his, so Moses did his, so Paul did his. The service that Noah did would not have been proper, nor suitable in Moses in his generation, nor Moses in David's, nor any of them in Paul's. Several persons have their several particular generations to serve in.

Thirdly, that particular generation which every person is to serve in is allotted him by the counsel and will of God; For David after he had served his own generation by the will of God; it is not by chance that men are cast on the generation they live in; men are not thrown into the world by God as we cast counters out of a bag, neither knowing nor regarding which comes first, which last. No, God who does all things in number, weight, and measure, he, from eternity, has appointed and allotted to every man the age and generation he shall serve in, "He hath made of one blood all nations to dwell on the face of the earth, and hath determined the times before appointed, and the bounds of their habitations," (Acts 17:26).

Fourthly, it is a great honor to the greatest man on earth to be serviceable to and in his own generation. David though a King, yet this is spoken of him by way of praise and commendation, "He served his own generation."

Fifthly, it is a good man's honor to be serviceable to his generation his whole time. David served his generation, not an apprenticeship only, or three apprenticeships, as Jacob served Laban, but his whole time; he served his generation until he fell on sleep. His serving his generation was not like Tiberius his *quinquennium (five years)*.

Sixthly, the rule of our serving our generation must not be our own will, nor the will of men, but the will of God. For David served his own generation by the will of God.

Seventhly, there is a time when all our serving of our generation shall cease and we shall fall asleep. For David after he had served his own generation by the will of God, *fell on sleep*.

Eighthly, the death especially of the righteous and godly is a sleep.

Ninth, the time of men's sleeping the sleep of death is determined and appointed by God. David fell on sleep by the will of God.

Tenth, God will have his children serve out their generation before they die. It was not the will or counsel of God that David should die till he had served his generation.

Eleventh, men by death are laid to their fathers. *Eunt ad plures* was the heathen's phrase of death, *Eunt ad patres* is the Scripture phrase. David fell on sleep and was laid to his fathers.

Twelfth, and lastly, all that ever died or shall die (except the Lord Jesus Christ) all else, even the greatest and holiest must and shall see corruption. David, a King, yes, which is more, a saint, and which is yet more, a prophet, yet he saw corruption. Only the Lord Jesus Christ, because he saw no corruption in the grave; because there followed no corruption of sin on the union of Christ's soul and body in his conception, there followed no corruption of body on the dissolution of that union. But David, after that he had served his own generation by the will of God, fell on sleep, and was laid to his fathers, and saw corruption.

So that you see my text, like Jacob, out of whose loins issued twelve sons; or like Elim, where the people of Israel met with twelve wells. Or the five particulars of this text are like those five loaves (of which you read in the Gospel) which being broken multiplied into twelve baskets full. I shall empty but one of these baskets for your entertainment at this time, and lead you but to one of these twelve wells for your refreshing, and that is the doctrine which is the fourth in order, and was laid down in these words. That it is a great honor to the greatest on earth to be serviceable to and in his own generation.

David, though a King, though a saint, though (in some sense) a king of saints, yet this is spoken of him in his praise, he served his (or in his) own generation. In the original the word signifies not a verbal superficial, complimentary service, such as our times abounds with the profession of, (your servant sir, is in every man's mouth) but a real, painful, laborious service. The Greek word most properly signifying one that takes pains and tugs at the oar. David found the Church and commonwealth of Israel in a crazy, leaky condition, and he labored hard and took pains to serve his generation, and to bring that weather-beaten bottom the generation was embarked in, into safe harbor.

The words used are (Acts 20:34) to signify to serve by way of relief: "These hands (the apostle says) have ministered to my necessities of his generation. In Acts 24:23 it signifies courtesies and offices of love, where it is said, Felix commanded the centurion to keep Paul, and let him have his liberty, and to, "forbid none of his friends to minister to him," to do any office of love to him. So David *did many offices* of love to his generation, and this was his praise and honor. This is engraved by the Holy Spirit on his tombstone instead of all other *Ecomiums*, he served his own generation. And this, every man no matter how great, should look on as his greatest honor, saying with Maximinius the emperor, *Quo major sum eomagis laborare cupio*, the greater I am the more work I desire to do. And make that his motto which was once the motto of the Prince of Wales, *Ich Dien (I serve)*.

You may consider David in a threefold capacity; first, in a private capacity, as a member of the Jewish commonwealth; secondly, in his policital capacity, as a King in Israel; thirdly, in his ecclesiastical capacity, as a member of the Church of the Jews; and in all these you shall find David doing eminent service and offices of love for his generation.

First, in his private, David served his own generation several ways; I will instance only in three, which are imitable and attainable by other private *persons:*

First, David as a private person served his generation by bewailing the sins and provocations of the time and age in which he lived. So, "Rivers of tears run down mine eyes because men keep not thy laws," (Psalm 119:136). David does not only now and then drop a tear, but mourns constantly, mourns impetuously, until his tears (like the waters in Ezekiel) swell into a river, and that (not only for his own sins, but) for the sin of others; for the sins of the times. And that was one special service and office of love done for this generation. So Lot was serviceable to his generation when he lived in Sodom, (2 Peter 2:8). So Ezra was serviceable to his generation, (Ezra 9:6). So Jeremiah, (Jeremiah 4:6). So the godly in Ezekiel's days, (Ezekiel 9:6). It is eminent service done in and to our generation to bewail its sins.

Secondly, David as a private person served his generation by making intercession and supplication for them, by thrusting himself into the gap and interposing himself between the wrath of God and the poor people. So, "Lo I have sinned and I have done wickedly, let thy hand I pray thee be on me and on my father's house," (2 Samuel 24:17). David here offers his own neck to the sword of divine justice to save the people. This was a powerful intercession, an excellent service done to his generation, on which the plague was stayed. David here did by the Angel, as the Angel did by Abraham, when Abraham had stretched out his drawn sword over Isaac to slay him, the Angel catches hold of his sword and stays his hand. So here the Angel had stretched out his drawn sword over Jerusalem to destroy it, and David comes and catches hold of the sword and stays the Angel and saves Jerusalem. This was excellent service done to his generation. Thus also Moses served his generation, (Exodus 32:31, Numbers 16:40). So Samuel, so Jeremiah, so Daniel, so Ezra, so the holy men of God from time to time have done service to their generation, (1 Samuel 12:23, Jeremiah 18:20, Daniel 9, Ezra 9).

Thirdly, David as a private person served his generation by walking before them in the example of a holy, unblemished, beautiful conversation. God, you know, everywhere gives this testimony of him, that he was a man after God's own heart. So eminently exemplary was the life of David for holiness and uprightness, as that it is made the standard and measure of the uprightness of others. And all that followed after him in the line of succession are reputed either good or bad, according as they walked or did not walk in the steps of their father David. David led the way and set the holy copy of a holy life not only to his own generation, but to the generations that succeeded after him. And so every godly Christian may and must serve their generation. Being, "harmless and blameless, the sons of God, without rebuke, in the midst of a crooked and perverse generation among whom you shine as light," (Philippians 2:15). Every Christian man and woman the worse the generation is in which they live, the better they should strive to be; that they might be as so many stars in a dark night, shining before others, and guiding their ways by the light of a gracious and holy example. So did David, and thus served his generation in his private capacity.

Secondly, in his political capacity, as a magistrate, as a King. David served his generation by administering judgment and governing righteously, "When I shall receive the congregation, I will judge uprightly," (Psalm 75:2). "I will early destroy all the wicked of the land, that I may cut off evil doers from the city of the Lord," (Psalm 101:8). So Phinehas also served his generation, "Then stood up Phinehas and executed judgment, and so the plague was stayed," (Psalm 106:30). David in the whole course of his magistracy served his generation by making the people's good the public good, the good of the generation in which he lived, the end of his government, and not his own pomp and grandeur. In which respect it is said of him, "That he fed (or governed) the people according to the integrity of his heart." (Psalm 78:72); by which he attained that happiness that few kings and princes that ever were in the world have had besides him. That the people found no fault at all with anything he did in his government. But, "whatsoever the King did pleased the people," (2 Samuel 3:36). Why? Because the people evidently saw that whatsoever the King did he sought their peace, and prosperity, and welfare in it. So he served his generation in his political capacity, as a magistrate.

Thirdly, in his ecclesiastical capacity, and as a Church member. David served his generation in the things of religion and of the worship of God. *For,*

First, where before the days of David Israel had been destitute of the Ark of God (1 Samuel 4:21): (the visible testimony of God's presence among that people, and so for their glory) the Ark had now for a long time been a stranger to Israel, and for a longer time had been a stranger to the tent and tabernacle, which was its resting place. David was the first man that made the motion for bringing back the Ark to the tabernacle of the Lord, (2 Samuel 6). And when they were discouraged in their first attempt by the breach which God made on them for a miscarriage and irregularity in that action, David's heart was so set on the work that he could not be taken off, but after a little pause he sets on it a second time and with a great deal of joy and triumph brings the Ark home to Jerusalem, though not without the slighting and scorn of his own wife, Michal.

Secondly, thinking it an unbecoming thing for himself to dwell in a house of cedar, when the Ark of God dwelt in curtains, (2 Samuel 7:3) he resolved with himself to build a house, a temple for the Ark of God to dwell in. And although God expressly forbade him to do this, because he had designed another hand for that work; yet such was David's love to, and zeal for religion, that he prepares all materials needful for so magnificent a work, "Now I have prepared (says he) with all my might for the house of my God, gold and silver, and brass and iron, and wood and onyx stones, and stones of diverse colors, and all manner of precious stones, and marble stones in abundance, (2 Chronicles 29:2-3). So David, as a member of the Church served his own (and after) generations in the things of God, in the promoting of religion and the worship of God. And so Ezra and Nehemiah, so Zerubabel and Joshua served their generations.

Yet further, David as a man extraordinarily inspired by God, served his generation by composing Psalms to be sung publicly in the worship of God, which are on record as parts of Holy Scripture, and by methodizing and regulating the worship of God as to the courses of the priests and Levites, and the several offices that each of them were to attend on in their courses, (1 Chronicles 23). As also by drawing up and delivering unto Solomon the scheme or platform of the temple which Solomon was to build. All which things referring to the worship of God, David took on him to order, not simply as he was a King, but as he was a prophet, one extraordinarily and infallibly directed by God in these particulars, as may be collected from 1 Chronicles 18:12, where it is said, "That David had by the Spirit the pattern," and again, "All this," says David, "the Lord made me understand in writing by his hand on me," (verse 19). So that this precedent of David may not be drawn in *Exemplum* by other godly princes; and it is (*pace tantorum virorum dixerim*) a mistake in some who would give unto the magistracy a kind of a supreme and legislative power *in sacris* (which is indeed the sole prerogative of Jesus Christ) from this example of David. But unless all magistrates had the same extraordinary Spirit and office that David had, they may not presume to do as David did. And yet princes and magistrates have enough still in David's example to imitate and to serve their generation. He in all his capacities, private, public, civil, religious, served his generation with the utmost of his abilities, ordinary, extraordinary; O that others would do so! It would certainly be their praise and honor as it was David's here. It is an honor to the greatest on earth to be serviceable to and in his generation.

And it must necessarily be so, because that man who serves his generation does good, and makes it his design to do good, not to some few, but to many, yes, to all, so far as it is possible for him in his sphere and capacity to attain. And by this first, evidences the richer stock of grace. Secondly, fulfills the end of his creation. Thirdly, comes nearest those beings which are most excellent; and all this is honorable.

First, (I say) such a man as serves his generation, the more service he does, the richer stock of grace and goodness he evidences himself to be in; *Bonum quo communius co melius.*

That conduit that is able to water a whole city, certainly has a more full spring than that which can supply only one street. The sun which serves all the world with light certainly has more fullness of light in it than ten thousand candles set up all at once. So here, that man that can do good and be profitable and serviceable not only to himself (Job 22:21), to his own family and kindred, but to the whole age and generation he lives in; that man has a rich spring and fountain of goodness in him. Certainly it is a great honor to such a man.

Secondly, such a man in some measure fulfills the end of his creation, which is to glorify God in being good ourselves, and doing good to others, to all as much as in us lies. And this is the very heathen could see. *Non solum nobis nati sumus sed partem patria.* And therefore the more generally and universally serviceable any man is in his generation, the nearer he comes to the end of his being, *yes.*

Thirdly, the nearer he comes to those beings which are most excellent. There is nothing in the whole visible creation more excellent than the sun in the firmament; nor nothing more serviceable, giving light, and warmth, and influence to all the creatures under heaven. Among all the creatures of God, visible or invisible, none more excellent than the angels; no, nor none so serviceable, "Are they not all ministering spirits, sent forth to minister for the good of them that believe?" (Hebrews 1:14).

Fourthly, yes, the Lord Jesus Christ himself, who (as man) is the first begotten of every creature, higher than the angels, yet he took on him the, "form of a servant," (Philippians 2). And professes, "that he came not to be ministered unto, but to minister," (Matthew 20:28). Yes, and now that he is in heaven exalted to the highest top of, "majesty and glory, far above all principalities and powers, every name that can be named," yet still he continues the, "Minister of the elect." And (with all humility and honor to his blessed majesty be it spoken) serves them as their High Priest, making continual intercession to God for them.

Fifthly, yes, God himself as he is *Primum and Optimum*, the first and best of beings, so he is the most communicative: "He gives to all life and being," (Acts 17:23, 28). "He upholds all things by the word of his power," (Hebrews 1:3). "He is good, and doth good to all," (Psalm 145:9). And therefore the more generally and universally good and useful any man is, the more like he is to angels, the more like to Jesus Christ, the more like to God himself. It cannot therefore but be a great honor for any man to serve his generation, which is to be a common blessing, a public good, and so to be like God himself.

I have given you briefly the explication of the point, I now come to the application of it.

And here I might in the first place take up a bitter lamentation, or rather reprehension against multitudes amongst us that are very faulty in reference to this great duty of serving their generations.

First, there are some that live wholly to themselves, minding only themselves and their own private good and interest. All their cares, thoughts, studies, affections are confined to themselves, centered on themselves; they do not mind, nor regard the good of the age and generation they live in; they do not care how things go in public, sink or swim, so they may abound in ease, wealth and prosperity; all their care is to enrich themselves and greaten their families. Mark what the Holy Spirit says of such a man, "Their inward thought is, that their houses shall continue forever, and their dwelling places to all generations," (And that is all they take thought and care for, and therefore,) they call their lands by their own names," (Psalm 49:11-13,16); as if they made account by this device to immortalize their names, and consecrate them to eternity, as much as if they had been the most serviceable men that the earth ever bore. But what says the Holy Spirit? "Nevertheless (for all their calling their lands by their own names) man being in honor continueth not. He is like the beasts that perish," (verse 12). He perishes and his memorial is perished with him. "His remembrance shall perish in the earth, and he shall have no name in the street," (Job 18:17). "This way is their folly," (verse 13). Whatever it is in the eyes of men, it is mere folly in the sight of God for any to think to perpetuate their names by heaping up lordships, and manors, and towns, and calling them by their own names, so their way is their folly. Yet their posterior (as very fools as themselves) approve their sayings, tread their steps. Against this folly the Holy Spirit gives the godly a caveat, "Be not thou afraid when one, (that is, such an one as he had been speaking of before, one that seeks not the good of his generation, that seeks nothing but to greaten himself and his family. Let it be no temptation to thee when such an one) is made rich, when the glory of his house increaseth. For when he dyeth he shall carry nothing away. His glory shall not descend after him. Though while he lived he blessed his soul, (saying with that fool in the parable, Soul, thou hast much goods laid up for many years, take thine ease, eat drink and be merry. Yet none blessed him.) And men will praise thee when thou dost well to thyself.", "Men," that is, some men, "will praise thee," flatter you, "to thy face when thou dost well to thyself," yet he that does not serve his, "own generation, shall go to the generation of his fathers, he shall never see light."

Secondly, there are others who are so far from serving the age and generation in which they live, they serve themselves of the age and generation *they live in*. These are such as make an advantage to themselves of the troubles and calamities of the times in which they live, and build their own nests on the public ruins. These, instead of serving their generation, are the plague and scourge of the generation they live in, "Woe unto him that buildeth a town with blood, and establisheth a city by iniquity," (Habakkuk 2:11).

Thirdly, again, others instead of serving the generation in which they live, they are the shame, the burden, the reproach, *Ulcus et carcinoma*, the scab, the plague of the generation they live in. Such are all profane ungodly persons, drunkards, swearers, adulterers and the like. How do these serve the generation they live in? Or what do these serve for? But only to poison and infect the age in which they live with their vicious conversations, to fill up the measure of its iniquities, and make it run over, and to hasten the wrath and vengeance of God on themselves and the age they live in.

But I had rather spend that little time that remains in a second use; and that is to exhort every one of you, seeing the greatest honor that the greatest on earth can have is to serve his generation, O be exhorted to lay out yourselves, your utmost, your all for the service of your generation. Whatever God has blessed you with, devote it all to his service, and the service of your generation.

Has God blessed you with able parts? Lay them out for the service of your generation; so did David use the extraordinary gifts of the Holy Spirit which he had received.

Has God blessed you with able purses? Do not grudge them to the service of your generation. David did not, but, "prepared with all his might" silver and gold, *etc.* for the building of the temple.

Has God given you power, interest, authority in your generation? Improve that for the service of your generation; so did David his. Serve your generation in your private and personal capacities, every one of you. And such as God has set in public places, serve your generations in your public capacities. First, serve your generation in your private and personal capacities.

First, by bewailing the sins of the generation you live in; that you may all do, and that you should do. And never did any generation call for tears more than ours.

Secondly, serve your generation by standing in the gap; by pleading with God to turn away his wrath from this generation. Never more need than now, never fitter opportunities than now.

Thirdly, serve your generation by the example of a holy and Gospel-becoming conversation. Never was that more needful than now, when the woeful miscarriages of many professors of the Gospel have made the very Name of the

Gospel and the reformed religion to stink in the nostrils of the nations that are around us, and have hardened the hearts of many amongst ourselves. O now labor to shine as lights in the midst of a crooked and perverse generation.

Especially those of you whom God has set in public and eminent places, in the magistracy and in the ministry, set you as lights in a candlestick, stars in a higher orb. O how should you willingly (with the apostle), "spend and be spent" in the service of your generation, (2 Corinthians 12:15). One of the German princes took for his device a candle burning in a candlestick with this motto, A.S.M.C. *hoc est, Aliis Servio, Meipsam Consumo*; I serve others, and spend myself. So should everyone whom God has set in public places say and do, even spend himself in serving his generation. To move you to this, *consider,*

First, it will be an honor to you in life, in death, and after death; yes it will be a comfort to you at the day of judgment and when you come in heaven, that you did not spend your days in vanity, that you did not live *telluris inutile pondus*, but served your generation.

Secondly, consider that you have only a little time to serve your generation in. It is but a span but an inch of time that you have to do service in.

Thirdly, consider that there are but few that seriously and conscientiously attend this work. We may take up the complaint of the apostle, "All seek their own," (Philippians 2:21); or that of Rabbi Simmeon, *Nathanielies F. Dies brevis & opus multum & operarii pauci, es merces multa & paterfamilias urget.* The time is short, the work is great, the laborers few, the wages ample, the Master urgent, therefore *Dum vires annique siunt*, while time and strength serves, serve your generation.

Fourthly, consider that the number of those who serve their generation diminishes and decreases daily. God has lately taken away not only in other parts of the nation, but here in Essex many excellent and serviceable ones in the magistracy and in the ministry. Men that were public blessings. And now last of all his faithful servant, the Reverent Pastor of this place, Mr. Samuel Collins, whose exceeding eminent serviceableness to and in his generation, I think, envy itself cannot deny, I say it again, envy itself cannot deny but that he was a man exceedingly serviceable in his generation; if any should, the stones of this place, yes, the stones of your streets and the walls of your houses would confute them. For who was the instrument, under God, of laying the foundations of religion and godliness among you? Was it not Mr. Collins? Who was the means of directing you into some kind of order and form, as it were, of civil government in this town, and thereby into a way of more vigorous suppressing disorders, and more comfortable providing for your poor than is almost to be found again in any town in the county? Who laid the platform of these things amongst you? Was it not Mr. Collins? Who was the occasion of building many houses (and as I have been informed, some whole streets in your town) by increasing the number of your inhabitants? Was it not Mr. Collins? The sweet sound and savor of whose ministry invited many from other places to come and seek habitation among you, so that whatever he was to others, yet it cannot be denied but he was to you, a man serviceable in his generation.

Nor can it be denied that he was serviceable to others also. His usefulness was not confined to one, but diffused itself into many places. Not to speak of the good he did by his own sermons preached abroad, how many congregations have cause to bless God for him, on the behalf of those faithful and godly ministers, which he procured to be sent to them, by the interest he had in those persons of worth and honor to whom by present laws, the *Jus patronus*, belonged?

Yes, how many have cause to believe God for the ministers that were brought up in his family, under his eye, care, and tuition, who have since proved eminent and worthy instruments in the Church of Christ? I think scarcely any man now living in England was more serviceable or happier in this kind than he.

And I could have wished (had it been the good pleasure of God) that this employment that is now cast on me, had fallen on the hand of some of them to whom this Reverent father might have said as aged Paul does to his beloved son and scholar Timothy, "But thou hast fully known my doctrine, manner of life, purpose, faith, longsuffering, charity, patience, persecution which came to me at Iconium, at Antioch, at Lystra, what persecutions I endured, but out of them all the Lord delivered me," (2 Timothy 3:10). I would this work had fallen on the hand of some of these who might have been *Testes Domestici & quotidiani*, daily and domestic witnesses of his conversation among you.

For my part I was but a child when he was in strength and glory of his ministry. But this much I remember, that when I was a child, Mr. Collins of Braintree was among those men, those ministers, whose names God had made precious among his saints.

Since I came to man's estate it has been my unhappiness that I have been almost a stranger to him, having opportunity only to give him seldom and short visits. But what I have learned either by my own observation or by the observation of others, that I shall not spare to speak; not so much to his praise as to the praise of God, from whom comes every good gift, and every perfect gift. And I do not know better what particulars to instance in then those, concerning which when Paul appeals to Timothy, "Thou hast fully known my doctrine, manner of life, *etc.*"

The first thing I shall instance is in his doctrine. As Demosthenes said pronunciation was the first and principal thing in an orator; so doctrine is the first and principle thing in a minister. I shall therefore first begin to speak of that.

I had the happiness sometimes to be his hearer; once (I remember) some twenty years ago, drawn by the fame of the man, I came a journey (of many miles) to sanctify a Sabbath here, and to enjoy his ministry, when I neither knew him nor any in this town, nor he, nor any here knew me either by face or name; and I received a great deal of satisfaction from the doctrine I heard from him then, and so I have done as often as I have had opportunity to hear him since. And I appeal to you who have been his hearers (as I think some of you have been) all the time of his going out and coming in among you, was not his doctrine always sound? Did he (in all the forty six years of his ministry among you, did he) ever broach any error, or vent any one heterodox or private opinion? No, was he not always a strong and zealous opposition of them? You that were his gravest and most judicious auditors speak, and I know you will say his doctrine was always sound; yes, and not only sound, but profitable, powerful, successful. Witness those many souls that God gave in to his ministry, and by his ministry in to Christ, some of which are now in heaven blessing God with him and for him; others are yet living in New England, and some I hope are yet living in Braintree, who must (if they will not be unjust and unthankful) say, that though they had many instructors, yet in Christ Jesus this was the man that begat them to God through the Gospel. His doctrine was powerful and successful.

And in this doctrine he was diligent, painful, laborious, and constant. For forty years together and above he preached ordinarily thrice every week, besides his sermons preached abroad, and occasional sermons at home. And even to this last winter (until it pleased God to give him a *supersedeas* by that sore sickness which at length served him with a *Quietus est* in death; until then, I say) he continued to preach constantly and ordinarily twice every Sabbath day. I profess that I have wondered that he had strength of body to do it, being almost fourscore years old, and that he had liberty of Spirit to do it, his ministry (even his) meeting with the same disrespect and discouragement that the labors of the rest of God's ministers generally meet with in these sinful, slighting, unthankful days. But God had vouchsafed him in a singular blessing, that even in his old age he was, "fat and flourishing," (Psalm 92:14). His understanding, invention, memory, utterance and other ministerial parts, they were as lively, as fresh and nimble now in his old age as in the prime of his years (at least I may say they were more fresh and lively in him than in many of us who are far younger men), that as it is said of Joseph, "His bow abode in strength." It is recorded of Moses as a singular and memorable thing, that when he was one hundred and twenty years old, his eye did not wax dim, and his natural strength was not abated, (Deuteronomy 34:7). And is it not as rare and memorable concerning this faithful servant of God, that when he was almost one hundred years old, lacking twenty, the eye of his understanding did not wax dim, nor his spiritual strength abated? But I see I must not bestow this much time in engraving every piece of this good man's character. I proceed therefore to the next mentioned by Paul, and that is his life, "Thou has fully known my doctrine, life, *etc.*"

Second, the life and conversation was not only unblameable and without rebuke, but holy, exemplary, and edifying. He was none of those that did with the stoics, speak well, but do ill, having Jacob's voice, but Esau's hands. He was none of those *Statua mercuriales*, that serve only to point others the way to heaven, but never move one foot in that way themselves. But as he preached so he lived; his doctrine was the rule of his life, and his life as the example of that doctrine. I may say of him as Bernard does of Humbertus, *Factitium vobis sermonem in omni fama sanctitatis servus Dei exhibuit.* This servant of God gave you a practical sermon continually during his whole conversation.

Third, and this his life and conversation declares what his purpose, his entering the ministry was (which is the third thing there mentioned by Paul), his purpose was not to seek great things to himself; no, no. You cannot but know what time was when the stairs of preferment were of as easy and open access to him, as they are now to some others. And though he never sought preferment, yet preferment sought him. And if places of greater eminence and greater profit could have tempted him, Braintree had never enjoyed his labors so long, nor been able to bewail his loss now; But as Gregory Nazianzen preferred his little village where he was Pastor before populous and eminent cities, so he this town of Braintree. He was resolved, *Hanes partum ornare.* He had purposed, resolved, and devoted himself, a servant of the Lord Jesus Christ, and your servant for Christ's sake; you were in his heart to live and to die with; you were his first, his only love. O that none of you had ever given him cause to complain with the apostle, the more abundantly I love the less I am beloved. In reference to this holy man, and what befell him in this congregation, I have often thought on that in Exodus, where it is said, "There rose up another generation which knew not Joseph." O, sirs, if you had all known (as some of you did) what service he had done for this poor town, what a state when he came first came here he found Braintree in, and what a state and degree of eminence in profession and outward prosperity he (or rather God by his means and ministry) had advanced it to, I am confident you would all have paid him the just tribute of love and honor at his death, which many of you did and do.

I go to the next particular and that is faith, "Thou hast fully known my doctrine, manner of life, purpose, faith." He was none of those, *Qui frigide & Jejune de fide differant*, that discourse of faith unto others coldly and overly, *Tanquam de terra incognita*. But as Tertullian speaks of the prayers of the primitive Christians, so it is true of his preachings, they were *tanquam de pectore*; his sermons came from the heart, he was a preacher that could say with the Apostle John, "That which we have seen with our eyes, and have looked upon, and our hands have handled of the Word of life, declare we unto you," (1 John 1:1).

The next thing the Apostle instances in is longsuffering. Now the longsuffering of this holy man, if it were not sufficiently tried in the time of his health, if the forty six years of time of his ministry in this place, and the variety of trials he met with in that time from men of several tempers and spirits; if that were not trial enough of his longsuffering, yet the many weeks of his sore and tedious affliction was. For many weeks was the hand of God heavy on him in a sore *Quartane Ague*. And in all that time he never uttered one unbecoming word, but lay quiet, contented, cheerful in the frame of his Spirit all the time of his sickness, until it pleased God to put an end to his days. Here was longsuffering. For his charity, though I say nothing, I am sure there are enough who will proclaim it. I believe there is scarcely a poor man or woman in all your town but will acknowledge that in him they have lost one of their best friends, one of their most ready, cheerful, tenderhearted relievers of their necessities that they had in all the world.

There is one thing more in these ministerial perfections summed up by the Apostle, and I know that some of you want to hear what I will say of that, and that is patience. And may I speak the truth, I never heard anything laid to the charge of this holy man in all my days but some defect in this particular, some want of patience. Now suppose that this charge were true, why? May not the want of this one particular grace be overlooked where there is such a full confluence of other graces? What man, what saint is there living on the face of this earth, that wants nothing? This holy man of God (some say) lacked patience; and are there not other men that want the wisdom he had, the gravity that he had, the sobriety that he had in the use of meats, and drinks, and apparel, the charity that he had, the modesty and humility that he had? And yet all these can be overlooked in them, only this one want of patience must be objected against him. But I beseech you, tell me (some of you) what was this lack of patience and in what cases? For there are cases in which to lack patience is not a fault, but a duty. There are cases in which good men, holy men may not be patient, cannot be patient, ought not to be patient. Even Moses himself, the pattern of patience, the miracle of patience, having to do with a forward and gainsaying people, has much ado sometimes to keep the bounds of patience, yes, he meets with some occasions in which he dares not but show some impatience. If the people in his absence set up a golden calf and worship it, patience can hold no longer; then how impatient would Moses have been if this had been done in his presence and before his face? If the people despise and loathe the manna of the Lord, if Cora, Dathan, and Abiram will rebel against the Lord by taking to themselves an office about the holy things, to which the Lord has not called them, and so make a schism, a sedition among the people; Moses cannot, must not be patient in these cases. Now I beseech you, what were the cases in which this servant of the Lord showed any impatience at any time? Were they properly his own concernments? When people withheld his maintenance from him was he impatient then? Did he molest any? Did he hail them before the Judge? When people despised him, opened their mouths in scornful, reproachful manner against him (as many delight to do against all the ministers of Christ Jesus) was he impatient then? Being reviled, did he revile again? Surely no. But if when he saw people slighting the precious manna of the Word, setting up the idols of their own brain instead of God's ordinances, sowing schism and division among the people committed to his charge; if on such occasions as these, his spirit was stirred in him, shall this be imputed as a fault to him?

This leads me to the last thing, persecutions and afflictions which he suffered. Not from the hand of public power; from that his own integrity and prudence, and (principally) that hand which upholds the stars in his Church, preserved him all his days under all that variety of changes that have passed over us. But I mean persecutions and afflictions from private hands. Not at Lystra, Iconium, and Antioch; not among heathens and Jews, but...I will draw a curtain here. The Lord has now delivered him out of them all; and I will not make these wounds *recrudescere*.

The Lord look on this poor town in mercy, and overlook all the failings and miscarriages of his people in it; and send a man among you (if it be his good pleasure) that may continue as long with you as this holy man did. And may do as much good among you as he in his generation; that though he find you divided, may unite you, and may restore you to your pristine state of beauty and unity, with which God had sometimes dignified you. Amen. *Amen.*

THE CRAFT AND CRUELTY OF THE CHURCH'S ADVERSARIES

Discovered in a sermon preached at St. Margaret's in Westminster, before the Honorable House of Commons, Assembled in Parliament. November 5, 1642.

By Matthew Newcomen,
Minister of the Gospel at Dedham in Essex.

Quid facit in Pector; Christiano Luporum Feritas, Canum Rabies, Savitia, Bestiarum, Vencnum Lethale Serpentum? Cyprian.

Cum sitis Impii Crudeles, Homicida, Inhumani, non amplius eritis Christiani, Lucifer Calazit.

Published by order of the House of Commons.

LONDON,
Printed for *Peter Cole*, and are to be sold at his shop at the *Sign of the Glove* and *Lion in Cornwall* near the *Royal Exchange*, over against the conduit,
1643.

IMPRIMATUR

Die Sabbathi, November 5, 1642.

Sir William Massam is appointed to return thanks to Mr. Newcomen, for his great pains taken in the sermon he this day preached at St. Margaret's, at the entreaty of this House, and to desire him forthwith to print his sermon, and to give a copy thereof to the committee for religion, that when they shall have the liberty to sit, they may consider by it, how to prepare and provide for the extirpation of popery; And it is further ordered, that he shall have the usual privilege for printing his sermon.

Hen. Elsynge, Cler. Parl. D. Com.

INTRODUCTION

To the Honorable, the House of Commons now assembled in Parliament.

If there is any history in all the book of God that may parallel our times, sure it is this of *Nehemiah.*

The people of Israel though delivered from their long and sorrowful captivity in Babylon, yet it was long that they could see truth and peace established in their Church and Commonwealth, the temple of God re-edified, the worship of God restored, the walls of the holy city repaired, the Lord's Sabbath sanctified, the Priests in their several orders and stations attending the service of their God. It was long in that matter of Church and state attained to a beautiful regularity. Some reckoning a 100. Others above 150. Some 200 years. Three onsets were given to this great work. Three times the Lord raised up and employed blessed and glorious instruments in it, before it arrived at its perfection. The first was Zerubbabel, (Ezra 1); the second was Ezra, (Ezra 7); the third was Nehemiah, the author of this book, who according to the good hand of his God on him, with invincible courage and indefatigable patience against the insolent scoffs; multiplied conspiracies and terrifying reports of his enemies, against the treacheries of some of his own brethren and nobles, and their base compliances with the public adversaries against the murmurings of the people, with great expense of his estate and hazard of his life, carried on this great work, and gave it a full and blessed period, to the comfort of the Jews and terror of their enemies.

To parallel this, the people of England, though through the mercy of God they have been in a gracious measure delivered from the spiritual captivity of Romish Babylon, which our forefathers were enthralled in so long a time; yet now almost a 100 years have passed over us, since that first deliverance, and yet we do not see that purity of truth, that beauty of worship, that orderliness of administrations, that strength of discipline, as walls and bulwarks about this, our Jerusalem, which has been the desire, prayer, expectation of us and the ages that were before us.

God seems to me to proceed by the same steps with us, that he did with the people of the Jews, and has made three visible and memorable onsets on the reformation and restoration of his Church among us. The first by that famous prince, the miracle and glory of his people and age, Edward the sixth, of every blessed memory, whose beginnings though exceedingly hopeful and promising, were soon stopped by a countermand, as it were from the God of heaven, as Zerubabbel's beginnings were by letters from the King, (Ezra

4:23-24). Soon after the work was revived again by his dear and gracious sister, Queen Elizabeth, in whose hands the Lord caused the work to prosper to some further perfection, yet not unto that beauty and glory we hope our God intends to raise it to; therefore this third time has God raised up instruments for the advancing of his work, even yourselves, honorable and beloved; who, though you have met with the same oppositions in this great employment that worthy Nehemiah did. Malignant scoffs, bloody conspiracies, reports full of various terrors, desertions of some of your brethren, murmuring of not a few of the people. Yet in the midst of armies and changes, of oppositions and discouragements, have here with unwearied patience and undauntable resolutions, not without great expense of your estates and hazard of your lives, attended on this work now these two years. At the present to the great grief of all loyal and honest hearts, we see you in the same posture that Nehemiah and his assistants were, (Neh. 4:17). Everyone with one of his hands working, and with the other holding his weapon, a sad condition. Yet go on, the work of reforming the Church is God's, he called you to it, he will maintain and defend you in it, he will give perfection to it, God is not as man, that he should begin to build, and not be able to finish.

The suitableness of this history, to our times, invited my thoughts (upon summons received to this service) to look into this book; and see if there were not something that might fit the day, and the suitableness of that portion of Scripture, which is the basis of this ensuing discourse unto the day, concluded my thoughts on this text. My desire and prayer was that I might speak something that might give encouragement to yourselves in the great things you are to work for God. This latter part of my desire was interpreted by a fear of consuming too much of that time, which (though your piety could willingly have bestowed on the work of praise offering) yet the extreme necessities of state could hardly spare. This made me silence much of what I had prepared to speak, both in the explicatory and applicatory parts of the sermon. Which yet (seeing it is your pleasures to command what you heard to the press) waits now with the rest on you. I dare not think there is anything, either in the one or the other, that can add to your light: if anything spoken or written may excite or increase your heat, I shall enjoy much of the end I propounded in this service. I do not dare undertake to direct anything, if in anything, I may erect your spirits in times so full of distempers, with a Christian and holy designation of all oppositions to carry on the great business of the Lord Jesus in establishing religion, reforming the Church, rooting out our popery, I have enough; if I fail of this, it is the sin of my infirmity, not by intention.

Luther in sad, tumultuous times was accustomed to say to his brethren and those about him, *Come let us sing the 46th Psalm.* I think you (Right Honorable) in these sad, conflicting times may say to one another, *Come let us read the book of Nehemiah*; there you may read experiences, encouragements, quickenings, directions, precedents; to spread all them before you is not the work of an epistle, nor is it needful, having been fully and excellently offered to your view in a *fast* sermon. Only this, as you have made the same preparations to this service you are now upon, which Nehemiah did, (Nehemiah 1), addressing yourselves thereunto by fasting and prayer. And have met the same varieties of oppositions and discouragements, so persisting in the same paths of zeal for God, compassion to his Church, dependence on his power; adherence to his cause, constancy in his service. Do not doubt but the same merciful hand of his and your God (after your Nehemiah-like conflicts shall crown your faithfulness with Nehemiah's successes; which were so glorious, that when all their enemies heard thereof, and all the heathen round about, they were much cast down in their own eyes, (Nehemiah 6:16); for they perceived that the work was wrought of God. And they that are of you shall build the old places, (Isaiah 58:12), shall raise up the foundations of many generations. And you shall be called the repairers of the breaches, the restorers of paths to dwell in, which has been, and is the prayer of,

The least and unworthiest of yours and the Churches servants,

Matthew Newcomen

THE SERMON

A Sermon Preached to the Honorable House of Commons now assembled in Parliament; November 5, 1642.

"And our adversaries said, They shall not know nor see, till we come in the midst among them, and slay them, and cause the work to cease," (Nehemiah 4:11).

This chapter gives you a view of the various discouragements, which that gracious man Nehemiah met in that glorious work of repairing Jerusalem, and restoring the lapsed state of the Church and Commonwealth. Discouragements you shall behold in this chapter, breaking in on him like waves of the sea while he stands as a rock unbroken, unshaken in the midst of all. Like Job's messengers, before the first is dispatched, there appears a second, before that can be answered, a third like Ezekiel's prophecy, mischief on mischief and rumor on rumor, (Ezekiel 7).

In the first verse, you have the adversary's rage, "When Sanballat heard that we built the wall, he was wroth, and took great indignation." In the second, you have this rage venting itself in foam, in scoffs, and sarcasms cast on Nehemiah, his brethren and their undertaking, "What do those feeble Jews? Will they fortify themselves? Will they sacrifice? Will they make an end in a day. And Tobias said, even that which they build, if a fox go up, he shall break down their stone wall."

But this is the coolest of their rage, the heat of it reaches to blood, so you find verse 7 and 8, "When Sanballat and Tobias, and the Arabians heard that the walls of Jerusalem were made up, they conspired all of them together to come to fight against Jerusalem and to hinder it." With it the people at the same time begin to murmur, verse 10, "And Judah said, The strength of the bearers of burdens is decayed, and there is much rubbish, so that we are not able to build the wall." And this (as it is probable) gives encouragement to the adversaries in antedate their triumph and glory, as if the Jews had been their conquest, their prey already, "And our adversaries said, *etc.*"

In which words you may be please to observe. First, a strong combination against the Church of God, "And our adversaries said." Secondly, a wicked design they were combined in, "To cause the work to cease," this is the first in their thoughts, though last in their words. Thirdly, a bloody means propounded, and agreed on for the accomplishing of that design; and that is slaughter: "Slay them, and cause the work to cease." Lastly, a subtle way projected for the effecting of that slaughter, "we will come on them secretly and suddenly, they shall neither know, nor see, till we are in the midst of them, and slay them, and cause the work to cease." I do not intend to prosecute the particulars of the text, but to give you the sum of the whole in one observation. The great design of the enemies of the Church, is by craft or cruelty, or both; to hinder any work that tends to the establishment, or promoting of the Church's good.

Doctrine. All the visible enemies of the Church of God are but the emissaries of Satan, his agents. And therefore they observe his (Ephesians 6:11) methods, his rules of art in their attempts on the Church. Now as Satan himself, sometimes opposes the Church by force, and then he is, "a piercing serpent," (Isaiah 27:16), and sometimes circumvents the Church by craft and then he is a crooked serpent, *vel draconem agit & fallis*. So do his auxiliary, those that fight under his colors against the Church's peace and good. Craft and cruelty are their chief engines of mischief. And not one but they use both, that as the Scripture speaks of those birds of prey and desolation, none of them shall want their mate. And as some write of the snake, he never wanders alone without his companions with him, so the craft of the enemies of the Church, is never but accompanied with cruelty, and their cruelty seldom without craft, and both bend to hinder any work that tends to the establishment and promoting of the Church's good.

To give you ocular proof of the cruelties by which the enemies of the Church have from time to time endeavored to cause the work to cease, would be the business, not of a sermon, but of a volume, and yet easily done, had we but time, because their cruelty ever appears in its own likeness, in the shape of one of those beasts that Daniel saw in his vision, "he had three ribs in the mouth of it, and they said unto it, arise, devour much flesh," (Daniel 7:5). You may trace the monster foot by foot from Abel to this present in steps of blood, the persecutions of the Jewish Church under Pharaoh. Nebuchadnezzar, Antiochius, and of the Christian Church under the heathen, and after them Arian emperors and Bishops since then under antichrist, on the one side and the Turk on the other, are so known, I need not mention them. But this they all declare, that the endeavors of the adversaries, have always been by cruelty to cause the work to cease. And indeed, if we consider those floods and seas of blood, which in the successive persecutions of the Church have been exhausted, we may wonder how the Church is not quite extinct, save only the blood of martyrs, *extra venas*, is not *cruor*, but *semen*, and by the irradiation of the sun of righteousness, becomes miraculously fruitful to the producing of a new succession of saints.

But to trace the adversaries of the Church in their craft, *hic labor, hoc opus*. They are *serpentine soboles*, the seed of the serpent; and as the way of a serpent on a rock is unknowable, so are their ways of undermining the Church. Yet as far as either in history or Scripture I may, I shall trace them, and give you a brief view of the several arts and craft, by which the adversaries of the Church have sought to hinder the proceedings, and cause the work to cease.

The first design that ever was against the Church, of which we read in Scripture, is that of Pharaoh and his counselors, "Come let us deal wisely with them," (Exodus 1); and what is the result of this consultation? Not to deny them presently the liberty of their religion, nor take away their lives, but by burdening and oppressing them in their liberties and estates, to break their hearts and imbase their spirits, that they should have no heart to mind religion or anything, because of their great anguish and affliction, a design that has been practiced against the Church of God many times. In this way the Persian tyrant thought to have subdued the spirit of Hormisdus, that noble Christian. He would not kill him, but enthralled him. Turn him out of his possessions, throw him from his honor, give his wealth, dignity, wife, to the basest of his slaves; turn him naked out of doors to keep mules in the wilderness, by this means, thinking to choke and smother that holy fire God had enkindled in his heart.

And this is the art of the great Turk at this day, though he pretends to let Christians in Greece and those countries

174

under him enjoy their lives and their religion, yet so heavy is his yoke on them, that they have little joy of their lives, and for the most part, as little care of their religion, scarcely anything more than the name of Christ generally to be found among them.

The second art by which the adversaries of the Church have sought to prejudice it, has been by procuring matches and mixtures of some of the members of the Church and some of their own that were idolaters. This was the art of Balaam, when he saw he could no otherwise fasten a curse on the Israel of God, he gave the King of Moab counsel to ensnare the men of Israel with the daughters of Moab, by which they were drawn, not only to corporal, but to spiritual adultery. The history of this you have stated, "The people began to commit whoredom with the daughters of Moab, and the people did eat of their sacrifices, and bowed down to their gods, and Israel joined himself to Baal-Peor," (Numbers 25:1-3). And that this was the plot of Balaam is clear, to commit trespass against the Lord; this was Balaam's counsel, and wicked counsel it was. This mixing with unbelievers, has been ever looked on as a thing of dangerous consequence to the Church of God; which is the reason that Nehemiah was in such a heat of indignation against the people for this thing, "I contended with them, and cursed them, and smote certain of them, and plucked off their hair, and made them swear by God, saying, you shall not give your daughters to their sons, nor take their daughters unto your sons; did not Solomon King of Israel sin by these things? Yet among many nations there was no King like him who was beloved of his God; Nevertheless, even him did outlandish women cause to sin," (Nehemiah 13:25-26).

The Church of God is exposed to great dangers by these designs. First, of being corrupt by this means, and drawn from the true religion, which is the very reason why God forbade marriages in the old law, "For they will turn away their sons from following me, that they may serve other Gods; so will the anger of the Lord be kindled against you, and destroy thee suddenly," (Deuteronomy 7:4). And sad experience of this sad effect and consequence of marrying with idolaters and those that are enemies to the Church, the Church of God has had, not only in Solomon, whose heart his idolatrous wives turned away from God, and so captivated, that he did publicly tolerate their idolatrous worship, "When Solomon was old, his wives turned away his heart after other gods," (1 Kings 11:4); and verse 7, "Then did Solomon build an high place for Chemosh the abomination of Moab, and for Moloch the abomination of Ammon:" and likewise, "did he for all his strange wives and sacrificed to their gods." Not only in Jehoram the son of Jehoshaphat, the reason of whose deflection from the practice of his father, and the principles of his education unto idolatry is rendered this by the Holy Spirit,

"For the daughter of Ahab was his wife," (2 Kings 8:18), not only in other of the Kings of Israel and Judah, but even in Christian Kings and Princes, when they have matched, though not with pagans and heathens, but with such as have professed the Christian religion, only not in purity. Valens, the Emperor was at first a true orthodox professor, but being married to an Arian lady, she soon ensnared him with her flatteries and captivated him to the same heresy with herself, and he proved a most bloody persecutor of the true orthodox Church.

Or secondly, if there is such establishment of the heart in the truth that the unbeliever does not dare attempt to draw the believing yokefellow from the true religion, or attempts it but in vain. This inconvenience yet follows on this, that the unbeliever will as much as they can, *vis & modis*, promote the false religion and subvert the true.

The Church of God had experience of this in Justinian the Emperor, whose wife Theodora, addicted to the heresy of Eutyches, did no less foster, encourage, promote, and reward the teachers and maintainers of that heresy than the Emperor did the true orthodox professors; yea prevailed so far with her husband, as to make Severus, a chief leader of the Eutychian faction bishop of Constantinople.

Thirdly, by this means not only the present age, but posterity is indamaged. For this case the unbelieving party survives, there is danger lest the children (especially if young) should by the authority of an idolatrous father, or the preservation of an idolatrous mother, be drawn away from the true religion. An instance of this we have in Valentinian the younger, whose father dying and leaving him in the tutelage of Justina, his mother, who was an Arian (though all the time of her husband's life she had concealed it knowing her husband's death, and the flexible age of her son to advance the Arian faction easily corrupted him, that he was scarcely warm in his throne but he falls when he persecuted the true religion. These and many other inconveniences have been observed to attend such kind of mixtures between the Church and their adversaries, which the adversaries are not ignorant of, to offer their daughters in marriage to the members of the Church, but it is only as Saul gave Michal to David, "that she might be a snare unto him," (1 Samuel 18: 21).

The third art by which the adversaries of the Church have endeavored the ruin and overthrow of religion, is by covering their intent to alter religion with a pretense of public emolument, so Jeroboam to cover his idolatrous projects, pretends the people's ease, "It will be too much for you to go up to Jerusalem," (1 Kings 12:28), a great journey, a great charge, you may serve God better cheap at Dan and Bethel; as if he meant not to alter religion, but only to let them have it with more ease and better accommodation. Like that of some

178

of late times. For people to hear two sermons a day, it is too much, one well heard and remembered is *enough*. For young folk to be kept from sports on the Lord's Day, it is too much, "It is too much for you to go up to worship at Jerusalem." The like pretense was sometimes used to Theodosius, justly called Great, who having abolished in Egypt their heathenish sacrifices, and forbid their idolatrous worship, upon pain of confiscation and death; the people fearing the omission of their accustomed superstitions, would make the River Nilus (whom they honored as a God) keep in his streams, and not water their land as in former years, began a mutiny, and things tended to sedition. Whereupon the President of the country, wrote to the Emperor, beseeching him, "for once to please the people, by conniving at their idolatry." To whom he answered, "It is better to continue faithful and constant unto God, than to prefer the overflow of Nilus, and the fruitfulness of the earth before piety and godliness. No, I had rather Nilus should never flow, than to have it raised by sacrifices and enchantments." A brave resolution, and becoming a true Christians Prince. Let people be pleased or displeased, come loss, come gain, let truth and godliness be maintained.

A fourth fraud or art by which they endeavor to supplant the Church is, by counterfeiting a friendly compliance with the Church of God, as if they were meant to help and farther the business thereof, when in truth, they intend nothing but to overthrow and hinder all. So the adversaries were like this in Ezra 4. When the people of God were about rebuilding the temple, the adversaries came and offered to join with them, "Let us build with you, for we seek your God as you do," (verse 2). When they intended nothing more than to betray them. This was the great art of the adversaries in the Apostles' days, when many false brethren joined themselves to the Church, merely to spy out their liberty. And many false Apostles that seemed to preach Christ with abundance of zeal and forwardness, but it was only that they might withdraw disciples from the true doctrine and Apostles of the Lord Jesus, and fill the Church with rents and schisms as they did the Church of Corinth. Thus the Arians would often counterfeit themselves orthodox and mingle themselves with orthodox professors, that they might with less suspicion spread the poison of their errors. That good Prince Constantine the Great, was abused much by that generation in this kind, his great admirer Eusebius confesses that he retained near him. *Sceleratos Nebulones ui simulaverunt Religionem Christianam.* Specially one notorious one, who had been chaplain to the emperor's sister, and by her dying, was commended to the Emperor, and receieved into his family, though all the time of Constantine the Great, he kept his poison hid; yet no sooner was he dead, but he began to play his pranks. First inveigling the chief gentlemen of the

Emperor's bed chamber, then some of the rest, after these the Empress, and soon after the Emperor himself; winning them all to the Arian heresy; who, if in Constantine's time he had not complied with the orthodox party, he had never had the access to Constantine, and so never this opportunity of spreading that heresy. This is a trick not unusual with Rome, I have heard that the Jesuits have a practice of running over the Lutheran Church, pretending to be converts, and to build with them, but it is only to keep up that bitter contention that is between the Calvinists and the Lutherans, the virulency of which, is much fomented by these renegade Jesuits.

The fifth way is, to ingratiate themselves to Kings and Princes, with much officiousness and pretended care of their profit and honor, that so being potent with the potentates of the earth, they may have the power to do the Church a mischief. So the adversaries of the Jews pretended that in duty and conscience they could do no less than complain of the Jews to King Artaxerxes, "Now because we have maintenance from the King's palace, and it was not unmeet for us to see the King dishonored, we have sent and certified the King," (Ezra 4:14). Wretches that cared no more for the King's honor than a straw, only pretend this, that they might the more easily draw out the King's power for the suppressing of the Church. So Haman seemed to mind only the King's profit, when his mind is only set on the Jews' destruction, "It is not for the King's profit to suffer them," (Esther 3:8). So the Jews themselves in prosecuting and murdering the Lord Christ, pretend nothing but, "loyalty and respect to Caesar, we have no King but Caesar. And if thou let this man go thou are not Caesar's friend." So that Arian priest, of whom I was even now speaking that corrupted Constantius the son of the great Constantine, insinuated himself first into the favor of that young prince by his officiousness, in carrying his father's will to him, and the advantage that he made of his favor was to corrupt and poison him. It has always been observed that the greatest heretics have been the greatest courtiers, the Arians in their age, and of them the Jesuits learned it, and of the Jesuits the Arminians learned it. All of them have made it their masterpiece to insinuate themselves into the favor of princes, and then make bold with their power, for the oppressing of the truth.

A fixed stratagem of theirs is to charge the truth and professors of it with false accusations, thereby to render them odious, either to princes or people. So the Gospel of Christ was called heresy, Paul a pestilent fellow and a mover of sedition. So, Ezra 4, the King is told if the Jews rebuild the wall, they will pay no toll, nor tribute. So the primitive Christians had horrible, unnamable crimes laid to their charges. Thus the Arians charged Athanasius with adultery, murder, and witchcraft. Thus the Jews of Persia, in the time of Saporet, accused Simeon, Bishop of Silencia, "as a friend of the Romans Emperors, and one that gave intelligence to them of the Persian affairs," which was the occasion, not only of the death of Simeon, but of a general persecution against the whole Church. In this way the Jesuits deal with the Protestants. And so the adversaries of the power of godliness; charge it with heresy, faction, rebellion, and all that will make it odious, either to prince or people.

The seventh way, is by procuring and enacting laws, by which they may either ensnare the consciences, or the lives of the people of God unawares. Such as that was when they came and told the King, "All the presidents of the Kingdom, the Governors and Princes, Counselors and Captains, have consulted together to establish a royal statute; That whosoever shall ask any petition of God or man, save of thee O King, for thirty days; shall be cast into the Lion's den," (Daniel 6:7). Darius was newly ascended on the throne, and his princes seemed to have studied nothing, but the increasing of his power and might, they pretend it will much add to his magnificence, and strike a greater awe into the hearts of his new conquered subjects, if such a law as this were made. Now when all the presidents, and counselors, and governors shall commend a thing to the King, as the unanimous result of all their counsels, and desire such a law to be made for the King's majesty and honor, it is easily obtained, though their design was by this law to ensnare the people of God, either to wound their consciences, by making them sin, in neglecting that duty of worship they owed to God, or else to cut off their lives in the pursuance of that worship. The King could not find this out, nor it may be most of the common sort of the Jews; but Daniel did, and resolved rather to, "transgress the laws of the King, than the law of God," rather to be cast into the den of lions, than to carry about a lion in his bosom, even an enraged conscience. So Julian, that subtle enemy of the Church of God, ensnared the poor Christians unawares, for calling his soldiers to appear before him, that they might receive their pay, he caused an altar with fire on it to be set by, and a table of incense, and commanded every soldier, as he came to receive his money, to cast some incense into the fire on the altar, which some of his Christian soldiers understanding to be an implicit and interpretative idolatry, refused to do, and would rather lose their pay. Others not knowing the depth and mystery of this iniquity, suspecting no hurt, did it, and so defiled their consciences; which filled them afterwards with such extreme grief and horror, when they came to the knowledge of it, as they did offer to expiate their sin with blood. Had Darius known that the intent of his princes, in that which they called their royal law, had been to entrap the life of Daniel, he would never have signed it. Had the

Christians known that the intent of Julian, in commanding
them to sprinkle some incense on the burning altar, had been
to make them deny the faith, they would have never done it.
But this is the craft of the adversaries, to procure and enact
laws, that may look one way and strike another, that seem to
be for majesty, honor, or decency, but are indeed for the
ensnaring and supplanting of the Church of God.

Another way is, by secret conspiracies, and
treacherous combinations against the Church, to undermine
and ruin it. So here, "The Arabians and the Ammonites and
the Ashdodites, conspire all of them together, to come and
fight against Jerusalem," (Nehemiah 4:7-8). So, "They take
crafty counsel against thy people, and conspire against thy
hidden ones, they have consulted together with one consent,
they are confederate against thee. Gebal and Ammon and
Amalek," (Psalm 83:3). So, "Certain of the Jews banded
themselves together, and bound themselves under a curse,
saying, that they would neither eat nor drink, till they had
killed Paul," (Acts 23:12-13). Such was the stratagem of our
adversaries, the deliverance from which we celebrate this day,
a conspiracy of men, that had bound themselves by a curse to
destroy us, and had not only said, but sworn, "We will come
on them, and they shall neither know nor see, till we are in the
midst of them and slay them, and cause the work to cease."
Their design was by craft, and truth is in reason we can look

for no other, if we consider the innate disposition of the enemies of the Church.

First, in regard of that implacable hatred the adversaries bear to the Church. It is a true saying, *Odia Religion sunt acerbissima*, hatred grounded in indifferences of religion are the most bitter and incapable of reconciliation. And it is a true observation of some that the nearer any are to a conjunction in matters of religion, and yet some difference retained, the deeper is the hatred; as he observes a Jew hates a Christian worse than he does a pagan or a Turk; a Papist hates a protestant worse than he does a Jew; and a formalist hates a puritan worse than he does a papist. No such hatred under heaven (he says) as that between a formalist and a puritan. Now truth being one, the true religion is one, add this, the possession and profession of the true Church, this enrages all the world against it, pagans, Jews, Turks, papists, formalists; that as they idolize their own religion and opinion, and seek to suppress each other, so they all combine to suppress the true religion, to keep that from flourishing, from shining forth in its original beauty and glory.

And then secondly ,they are full of craft; the seed of the serpent, for so God calls them, (Genesis 3:15) thereby letting us know, "that as the serpent was more subtle than any beast of the field," (Genesis 3:1). So the adversaries of the Church are more subtle than all the men of the world; whereas the

Church of God, they are the seed of Jacob, (Psalm 22:23). He was a plain man, *sine fraude and fuco* and so are his seed, *Prudetiam habent, fraudul entiam horrent*, but their adversaries they are full of craft, therefore sometimes in Scripture called *foxes*.

3. And as full of cruelty as craft, therefore in Scripture it is proclaimed as *bloody* as well as lions, bulls, dogs, unicorns, and wolves. The Church's enemies are men of cruel, bloody dispositions, such as was Francis the first of France, whose rage against the truth of God, and the reformation in Luther's time, was so bloody that he protested in a solemn assembly, "If he knew any part of his body infected with that contagion (Of Lutheranism) he would presently tear it from him, that in might spread no further."

Or that German Count, Felix of Wartenburg, who said he hoped he died, to ride up to the spurs in the blood of the Lutherans. These are the dispositions of them all, for as face answers face in water, so the heart of man to the heart of man. Now look on the adversaries of the Church thus, as full of innate craft, cruelty, malignity against the Church of God and the true religion, and what can you expect, but that they should by all deceitful, bloody ways, hinder and oppose any work that tends to the establishment and promoting of the Church's good.

But if you add to this, the mighty power that Satan has in the hearts of the Church's enemies, to every one of whom it may be applied, which Peter said to Ananias, "Satan hath filled thy heart," yea Satan has not only filled them, but as the Holy Spirit in one word tells us, is, "continually alive and mighty in them." And again tells us, they are as spontaneously subject to his power and motions. That native malignity, craft, cruelty, that is inherent in the Church's adversaries is principle enough to carry them on in designs against the Church's good, though Satan should never incite them; and that power and energy of Satan in them, is enough to carry them in that way, though there was no such natural disposition. But when both meet, a strong propensity of nature in themselves, and a mighty energetic power of Satan over them, they must with most impetuous violence be carried by any craft or cruelty, no matter what or how to hinder all that tends to the Church's good. They, having an activity of their own that way, and Satan who is mighty in them, acting them that way too.

It is true, God could restrain the rage of his Church's adversaries, bind down the malignity of their natures (though he leaves it in them) with a band of brass and iron, as the stump of the tree in Nebuchadnezzar's vision, and crush the devil's own malice. But it pleases the wisdom of God to give scope in this way to the malice of Satan and his instruments, and that both, in reference to his people, and to himself.

To his people. First, for their trial, the reason the Apostle gives, why the Lord permits heresies in his Church, may let us see why the Lord suffers other opposition against his Church, "There must be also heresies among you, that they which are approved may be made manifest among you," (1 Corinthians 11:19). Who will not own the Church's cause, when it prospers, meets with no opposition? The Samaritans were accustomed to challenge the kindred of the Jews, which the state of the Jews flourished, but when it was afflicted then it disclaimed them. Many will embark themselves in the Church's cause in a calm, that with the soldiers in the acts will fly out of the ship in a storm. Therefore that his own which are approved may be manifested, God suffers Satan and his instruments to oppose, to use all their craft and cruelty to hinder his Church's good.

And not only that his people may be tried, but also exercised in wisdom, faith, patience, courage. When there was deliberation at Rome about the demolishing of Carthage, let it stand, says Scipio, lest the people of Rome should want an occasion or object whereon to exercise their valor. God could soon annihilate his Church's enemies; but let them live, says God, let them do their worst, they shall but be for the exercise of my people's wisdom, faith, zeal, constancy, courage, and the whole panoply of grace.

And yet God has a further end in permitting this, than his people's exercise and trial, and that is the illustration of his own glory, by craft and cruel attempts of the Church's enemies, that the glory of his wisdom and power in the preservation and prosperity of his Church might be the more illustrious. Archimedes had never been so famous, if the city where he dwelt had not been so long, so violently besieged, and a long time preserved only by his means. If the Church of God, the city of the habitation of his holiness, should not often be surrounded with enemies, besieged with difficulties and oppositions, the wisdom and power of God, in preserving and prospering his Church, would never be so glorious, therefore the Lord suffers the adversaries of his Church to design and endeavor by craft or cruelty, or both, to hinder any work that tends to the Church's good, gives them leave to plot, and conspire against his Church, and lets them say, "They shall not know nor see, till we are in the midst of them."

And now, if ever a text were *verbum diei*, as the vulgar Latin reads it, or *verbum super rotas*, as some others. Surely this truth, this text is such. Every word of this text is a wheel of that triumphant chariot, in which our Church and state this day glories over a design of our adversaries against us, fraught with all the subtlety and cruelty that hell itself was able to infuse into it, this day thirty seven years, was this Scripture fulfilled in England.

This day thirty seven years, the King then sitting on the throne, had summoned the peers and commons of this kingdom to an assembly of Parliament. The intent of that meeting (as was hoped by God's people, and feared by their enemies) was to surround Jerusalem, and the temple, with walls and bulwarks, to secure the Church, the true religion and worship of God, with needful, healthful laws. This was the work intended. Wherefore should a Parliament meet, but for the work? And our adversaries said, "they shall not know, neither see till we are in the midst of them and slay them, and cause the work to cease."

Our adversaries. Who are they? Consider and then judge. Who are they that (when the time was) filled their loathsome prisons with the bodies of our forefathers? They made our land drunk with the blood of martyrs? In the space of less than 4 years they sacrificed the lives of 800 innocents unto their idols. And ever since God has put a stop to those bloody outrages, have travailed with nothing but England's destruction now these fourscore years. Who are they that have made so many deadly blows at the heart of the state? Who are they that have given life and vigor to so many insurrections and rebellions in the bowels of the kingdom? Are they not the *papists*? It is easy then to point out these adversaries. The papists, they are our adversaries, so they have been, so they are, so they will be, as long as Christ is ours, his

Gospel ours, and the reformed religion ours. Sooner shall a man find honey and balm in the nest of snakes and the dens of dragons then we true friendship and peace with papists. Sooner shall east and west meet and kiss, the ark and Dagon, Jerusalem and Babylon, Christ and Belial cease to be adverse, then they cease to be our adversaries. These were, these are, our *adversaries*.

And our adversaries said, these our adversaries had had many a saying to us, they had said in 1688, "Come and let us cut them off from being a nation, that the name of England may be no more in remembrance." They had said as Moab, upon Rome, to the spoil, presuming that the victory was theirs before the fight. And when that saying was disappointed, yet they said there was a day a coming, which should pay for all, that was the day of Queen Elizabeth's death, concerning which their *Balaams* prophesied, "That by the uncertainty of the next heir, the kingdom was in a desperate case, in the greatest misery that ever it was, since or before the conquest, and far worse than any country in Christendom, that clouds of blood hung over England, which waited but her dissolution for their dissolving, that on her death England would be a common prey, and her tomb would be England's grave. This our adversaries said then, and from these sayings issued that all prodigious variety of murderous people against the sacred person of that ever honored Queen, the miracle of her sex, the glory of her age, the astonishment of the world. But the silver line of her precious life, being hid in the hollow of God's hand from all their desperate assassinates, she full of years, and more full of honor, went to the grave in peace. And God who frustrates the tokens of the liars, and makes diviners mad, contrary to the hopes and confidences of our adversaries, brought in a peaceful King, and established his throne in peace.

What do our adversaries say now? Are they not so ashamed and confounded in their former disappointments, as they can open their mouths no more? No, they are saying still, the malice of our adversaries is incapable of disheartening, as Balaam was in his attempts of cursing Israel. Let God appear never so often against them, "let the Angel of God stand with a drawn sword in his hand...yet again," our adversaries said.

What Pharaoh said to his servants, that our adversaries said to one another, "Come let us deal wisely," our former projects against this people have been too shallow and open, our preparations in 1688 proclaimed our intentions, and made them frustrate, the treasons of Parry, Lopez, Sanders, *etc.* were common, ordinary, and poor attempts, now for some a rare *stratagem*, some depth of darkness, some mystery of unheard of treachery, that may be acted by unseen instruments, they shall neither know nor see, until we are in the midst among them. And what was this, but the event of the *powder treason*? Look on the cunning projecting and carrying on of that treason, you will hear our adversaries saying, "They shall neither know nor see, until we are in the midst of them." And look on their bloody intent in it, "And it was to slay, and cause the work to cease."

First, for the crafty projecting and managing the plot, because they will make sore, we shall know nothing, none shall be admitted to consultation about the thing, but those that by vows and oaths and sacraments, and all that is sacred, bind themselves more than once, neither directly nor indirectly, neither plainly nor by circumstance to discover the plot. Here it was that in two year's space (for so long was this treason forming) not the least inkling of it came to any of our ears, our adversaries had sworn, "They shall not know," and if ever they were true to their oaths, it was here, "They shall not know."

"Nor see." Therefore all their work lies underground, and it is dispatched in the night, when dead sleep falls on men. If either the darkness of the night, or the depth of the earth can hide it, we shall not see. And how did God for a while seem to smile on their project, and to facilitate their work, when providence offered the convenience of a cellar to them, where they thought they must have dug a vault by strength of hand, to lay their powder in. How did God seem to have cast this Kingdom and city into a dead sleep, so that 36 barrels of gun powder should be conveyed into a cellar so near the Parliament house, and a Parliament so near, and none have the least suspicion of treason? Could this have been if God had not stupefied men? God himself seemed to take their part, and they who not many years before had sworn God was turned Lutheran, began to hope, God was turned Catholic again. God seemed to have conspired with them, and to say, "They shall not know, nor see."

"In the midst of them." How? As Jesus in the midst of his disciples, saying, "peace be unto you." No. But as the enemies were in the midst of the congregation, "O God thy enemies roar in the midst of thy congregation." They made account to have come into the midst of them with such roaring as would have astonished the heavens, and made the earth tremble, "In the midst of them," as the daughter of Herodias was *only to suck blood*, "to slay them," that is the end why they would be in the midst of them. And our adversaries said, "They shall not know nor see, till we are in the midst of them and slay them."

"Slay them." Whom? The whole assembly of Parliament, and in this to quench the light, and extinguish the glory of the English nation. Never was any treason before this so destructive. Others were but petty treasons compared with this. This was the masterpiece of all the policy of Rome and hell. Unless it were the treason of Satan against the state of man in paradise, to blow up all mankind in Adam, the representative of it at once, no treason like to this. This was second to that, of which they say, as he sometimes of Goliath's sword, none to that, none to that, in which the flower of our Gentry, our whole nobility, the princes of the blood, the Lord's anointed, the royal seed were all devoted to one stroke of destruction. And our adversaries said, "They shall not know nor see, till we are in the midst of them and slay them."

"Slay them." Aye, such instruments of cruelty they had prepared for this slaughter, as no one of that assembly, could have fled from the fury of it, had they wings of Eagles, nor resisted the force of it, had their flesh been as brass, or their strength as stones, or their bodies armed with the scales of Leviathan. They were not swords, nor pistols, nor poisons, the ordinary weapons of Rome's warfares, but instruments more inevitably killing, 36 barrels of gunpowder, enough to have blown to dust, the strongest fort in Christendom. These were the instruments of their cruelty, such as were never found in the habitations of Simeon and Levi. With these they intended to come in the midst of them and slay them, and that with such a slaughter, as was never heard before. Show me in any history and precedent of the like slaughter as was intended here. Wicked Abimelech slew on one stone threescore and ten of Gideon's sons, yet one escaped. Jotham had his life saved. Bloody Saul cause fourscore and five of the priests of the Lord to be slain in one day, yet Abiathar, the son of the high priest, had his life given him for a prey. Ambitious Athaliah sought to destroy all the King's seed, yet Joash, the King's son was preserved. In the massacre of France, above threescore thousand slain, yet some escaped, even of those that were appointed to the slaughter. But here, O merciless cruelty, not one man that had escaped, neither King, nor Prince, nor Lord, nor any of that Honorable Assembly, though all of them, as Zeba said of the brethren of Gideon, were men, "each one resembling the son of a King;" yet they had all perished together in a moment, not one escaping. The devil dealt more mercilessly than this with Job, when he slew his sons and servants, he still left one alive to carry the tidings, but here all die or none. And that in such a crafty, sly way, as they shall never know who hurt them, "They shall not know nor see." No, the craft of our adversaries extended so far as to provide, not only to hide themselves from the sight of men, whom they intended thus to cut off, but from the rest of the nation. You know the ways they had taken to cast the odium of that horrid treason of the true Protestants, under the name of puritans, if God had not in mercy delivered us from that conspiracy, we had born not only the misery, but the infamy of it.

And our adversaries said, "They shall not know nor see, till we are in the midst of them, and slay them, and cause the work to cease." It is the work they were about, that is the cause of all their rage and malice. They were about to make laws for settling true religion, and repressing popery. And as Pilate came on the Galileans, when they were sacrificing, and mingled their blood with their sacrifices. And as the adversaries here made account to come on Nehemiah and his builders, and temper their mortar with their blood, so did ours plot to come on our lawmakers, they, "shall write no law, but in their own blood."

And O Lord, if this plot had taken; what a Vesuvius, what an Etna had this place been? What an Aceldama, what a Golgotha had this land been? What a chaos had this Church and state been? How had our laws, liberties, religion been swallowed up in that fiery gulf, and buried in those ashes. How would that man of sin, that son of perdition have satiated his thirst of blood in the achievement of this day, and have looked on those piles of mangled, dismembered bodies, and that horrid face of death, such as was never seen before, with as much content as Hannibal did on a pit full of the blood of men, when he cries out, *O formosum spectaculum.* Or Valesus the Asian Proconsul, when trampling over the carcasses of 300 men whom he had slain, he cried out, *O rem regiam.* Or that Queen, who when she saw some of her Protestant subjects lying dead and stripped on the earth, cried out, "The goodliest tapestry that ever she beheld." Many goodly bloody sights have antichrist glutted his cruel might with: the funeral piles of England in Queen Mary's day; the massacre of France; the war of Germany; the butchery of Ireland; goodly sights in the eyes of antichrist. But to have seen a whole Parliament, and in this the peace and religion of a whole kingdom, blown up in a moment! Thuanus writes, that the Pope caused the massacre of Paris to be painted in his palace; surely had this plot succeeded, it should have been portrayed in his holiness' chapel or oratory.

And how did it come to pass that it did not succeed? Was there anything lacking either in the wills or endeavors of our adversaries? No, our adversaries said, "They shall not know nor see, till we are in the midst of them and slay them." Nor did we till that very night, that morning the fatal blow should have been given. And then it was not in any state with vigilance or prudence, but merely divine providence that brought to light this work of darkness. The particular act of which providence I do not need to instance (where heretics were about to bomb parliament), you know the story, and all that know it will acknowledge that if ever the arm of God were revealed in any deliverance, it was in this; only that by all which has been spoken, our hearts may be raised to the higher strain of thankfulness, let me as I have set before you the subtlety and cruelty of our adversaries in the invention of this treason, present unto you the mercy of God in the prevention of it.

O how freely did God deliver us from the bloody intent of our adversaries. Many deliverances has God wrought for ourselves, for other Churches, for his Church in former times, but was there ever any so free as this? God delivered his Church from the bloody conspiracy of Haman, a work of astonishing power and mercy, (Esther 4:26). But what prayers, what tears, what fastings and wrestlings did it cost Esther and Mordecai, and the whole Church, that they could obtain that deliverance? It was a gracious deliverance God wrought for his infantile Church, in rescuing Peter from the hands of Herod, but it was wrought by abounding importunity, "incessant prayer, prayer was made without ceasing of the Church unto God for him," (Acts 12:5). But this deliverance did not come on the wings of our prayers, but God's free mercy, we did not know our danger, and therefore could not make deliverance the subject of our prayers. Masses were said in Rome, for the good success of the Catholic design, but no prayers in England for our deliverance from their treason, and yet were delivered, admirable mercy! This is a people to be delivered by their God, before they seek deliverance.

2. And delivered so fully. You know the plot was laid for a full destruction, to cut off every person in that honorable

assembly. To blow them all up, tear them all in pieces, and in and with them the whole nation. But see how fully God prevented their mischievous design; that not a limb of any one of them was shaken, not one bone broken. The deliverance was like that of the three children in the fiery furnace, "There was not so much as a hair of their head singed, neither did the fire so much as take hold on any of their garments, neither was there so much as the scent thereof on them." Like that of Jerusalem, from the fury of Sennacherib, who coming up against the Church full of pride and rage, intending nothing, but to break in pieces and destroy. God says, "He shall not come up against this city, or shoot an arrow there." So said the Lord to our adversaries, "You shall not come up against this assembly, nor fire one corn of powder, nor shed one drop of blood there," where they intended to have filled all with blood and fire, O admirable deliverance! Has God delivered Germany in this way? Is Ireland so delivered? O England, England! The ashes of Germany, the blood of Ireland, proclaim your deliverance this day, glorious in the fullness of it.

3. And not only in the fullness of our deliverance, but in the confusion of our enemies, whom God took this day in their own pits and snares. And the plot they had laid to blow us up, recoiled and blew up themselves. God turned it to their own destruction. That which they had designed for the advantage of their Catholic cause and (a good cause, and a

good religion, that must be advanced by such sinful, devilish ways) has been the greatest disadvantage to their cause. All the streams of Tiber will never wash off that blot of just infamy which this treason has fastened on them, till Babylon sinks like a millstone into the bottom of the sea, it will never be washed off; this was the Lord's doing. This turning the wheel on our adversaries, this bringing their mischief on their own heads, was the Lord's doing, and it is marvelous in our eyes.

But now as that great King, "When he read in the records of his Chronicles, that Mordecai had discovered a treason against the King," (Esther 7) presently inquired, "What honor and dignity had been done to Mordecai for this." So do you. You have seen this day a brief record of that which deserves a larger chronicle. You have seen how the God of heaven prevented and disappointed a treason as dark and cruel as hell, intended against the whole state and kingdom. Now it is your part (Honorable and Beloved) who representatively are the whole nation, it is your part to inquire, what honor, what dignity has been done to God for this.

It is true, that Parliament then assembled, whose the deliverance more immediately was, ordained this anniversary, which we celebrate this day. But besides this, what honor, what dignity has been done to God. What has been done for the advancement of his glory, the propagation of his Gospel, the repressing of popery from that deliverance unto this day. Do you in your consciences think that the bare keeping of this deliverance in memory, or as acknowledging of it in our assemblies, as at this day, is sufficient retribution of dignity and honor to our great deliverer. Did Hezekiah not do as much as this; did he not indict a song in the praise of that God, that delivered him from the sentence of death. You have it (Isaiah 38:10), yet it is not said, (2 Chronicles 32:35). But Hezekiah returned praise to the Lord, even a psalm of praise. But Hezekiah returned not unto the Lord, according to the benefit done to him. Therefore wrath was on him and on Judah and Jerusalem. May it not be said so of England for all our anniversaries, our sermons, and songs of praise, but England has not returned to the Lord, according to the benefits done unto them. *Quid verba audiam, facta cum videam.* Dare I say God, for the flattering praises of England, when I see the cursed practices of England! Have not my purest truths been adulterated in England, and Rome's grossest errors entertained in England, and that even since this deliverance? Have my purest ordinances been polluted in England and Rome's grossest superstitions practiced in England? Have masses not been openly celebrated with a greater confluence of multitudes to them, then to sermons and sacraments? (See Deuteronomy 32:6.) Have they not published edicts against the sanctification of my day, but none against the idolatry of the mass? Have they not without law, against law persecuted my ministers, my servants, imprisoning them, compelling them to voluntary exile, while they have neglected to put in execution their own laws against Romish priest and Jesuits. Do you thus requite the Lord, O foolish nation and unwise? Did I deliver you this day from Romish cruelties, that you should deliver up yourselves to Romish superstitions and idolatry? Is this to return to the Lord, according to the benefits he has done?

Arise, arise you princes of the tribes of England, you members of the honorable Houses of Parliament, act something this day, worthy of yourselves, worthy of this day, worthy of this deliverance, worthy of your great Deliverer. God (I persuade myself) has reserved to you the glory of returning to him according to this day's mercy. You have begun to do more for the repressing of popery, for the reforming of the Church in doctrine, worship, discipline, than your forefathers have done ever since the first hand was put to the work of reformation. Go on in the name of the Lord, in the power of his might, in the multitudes of his strength. Go on to root out not only popery, but all that is popish. Let this day add something towards the perfection of that work. Some such thing I suppose was in the hearts of the honorable Houses when they made choice of this particular day, if not to deliberate and advise something that might tend to the further honor of the Author of this day's deliverance and the farther confusion of the Author of the day's treason, the romish religion? Well, that assembly by the sad distempers of these bleeding times is yet suspended. I beseech you, make this the work of yours. And when you return to your Parliament House again, let the first question put to vote this day be David's, "What shall I render to the Lord for all his benefits towards me?" (Psalm 116) Let this be the question, and the God of wisdom and grace direct you in your resolves.

And whatever God shall reveal to make most for his glory, his Church's peace and good, the union of the kingdoms, the extirpation of popery, let that be the cowering act of this day. *Scipio africanus* being accused before the tribunes of the people, and the day of his trial falling on the same month and day in which he had some years before won a great victory over Hannibal, and on his first appearance addresses himself to the people in this way, *Hot die, Quirites, cum Annibale solicitor pugnatum est*, this day gentlemen did I fight with Hannibal with good success. Therefore leaving lawsuits, I pass directly to the capitol to salute the gods and give them thanks. *Hoc die Quirites;* this day, knights and gentlemen, God himself fought for you against Rome, O do not think it is enough that you have come to salute God in his temple this morning and give him praise; but when you return to your Parliament House again, letting all other businesses sleep a while, in the first place resolve this question, *Quis retribuam?* What shall I render to the Lord for all his benefits?

Application. And this I would rather excite you to (Honorable and beloved in our land) because, due thankfulness for former deliverances is a happy means to procure new. God is never weary of delivering a people that studies thankfulness. And has England not, has the Parliament no need of the arm of God to be stretched out again for their deliverance? For, do we now have no adversaries? Or have our adversaries changed their natures, put off their accustomed craft and cruelty, forgo their old note to say, "They shall not know nor see, till we are in the midst of them and slay them, and cause the work to cease?" No certainly, sooner shall the leopard change his spots or the Ethiopian his skin than adversaries change their crafty, bloody dispositions, or cease to plot ruin against us, until they have utterly ruined themselves by their own plots. Do you think our adversaries have been sleeping ever since this powder? Treason? You know what their molitions have been, and in your several remonstrances have made them known. Yet give me leave to inform the rest of our brethren a little of them.

Our adversaries in Ireland have been plotting their present rebellion these seventeen years as some have deposed.

These seventeen years have been making sure work and laying ground for the kindling of that combustion, which now devour that miserable kingdom. And what do you think our adversaries have been doing here the meanwhile, nothing? Where then proceeded those long intermissions of Parliament, that we began to fear our Parliaments would prove like those Roman solemnities, which no man lived to see twice, being held but once on a hundred years?

Where did the immature dissolutions come of so many Parliaments but from the plot of these our adversaries? He that does not know where the strength of England lies may learn of England's enemies, for as the Philistines, when they knew that Samson's strength lay in his hair, plotted to cut off that, and then they easily bound him, put out his eyes, and made him grind in their will. So our adversaries, knowing our strength to lie in our Parliament have been ever plotting to cut them off. One Parliament they attempted to blow up without powder, that set our Parliament's being intermitted, interrupted, they might at once lay blinds on us, and put out our eyes that we should not see our own bondage in our laws and liberties, and we should neither know nor see.

And if only in our laws and liberties, if as Esther said, we had only been sold for bondmen and bondwomen, the mischief would have been more tolerable. But had our adversaries not plotted to slay us, as the two witnesses were slain in Revelation? To slay us by taking the word of truth and life from us? Did they not say, we will come on them and they shall neither know nor see, until we are in the midst of them and cause that work to cease.

I know there are many in the nation (and may be, some here) that cannot be persuaded there was ever any, design for the alteration of religion amongst us. Such, I beseech in the spirit of meekness, to lend me a patient and unprejudiced care. I do not stand here to declaim against any persons or ranks of men. But to speak the words of truth and soberness, I know that I stand this day not only before a great court, but before a greater God, to whom I must give account for what I now speak.

Adam Contzen, a Jesuit of Menez in his second book of Politics, the eighteenth chapter, has drawn a plot for the cheating of a people of the true religion by sleight of hand, and the serving in of popery again on them by the art of slieght of hand, that they shall neither know nor see. The method of this (which certainly is one of Satan's methods) he lays down in certain rules. Be pleased but to observe, how exactly the late times have moved according to those rules, and then judge of their designs.

His first rule is this, to proceed as musicians do in tuning their instruments. Who strain their strings with a gentle hand and set them up little by little. Or as physicians do in curing diseases, who abate noxious humors by degrees and pauses. This rule was observed both for the destructive and abstractive way. For the destruction of the true religion, and the advancing of the false, they had learned this wisdom to proceed by degrees and pauses. And first for the destruction of true religion, to suspend all the orthodox preachers in the land at once, would have made too great a noise, therefore proceed by degrees. And first suspend all lecturers which will not constantly practice the ceremonies. Then alter a little pause, clap down all lecturers as an order of vagrancy, not to be tolerated in the Church. When that is done, forbid all Pastors and incumbents preaching in their own parish Churches on week days. Next, inhibit holiness on the Lord's day, in the afternoon, under pretense of advancing catechizing by that means, and yet within a little while, after forbidding all catechism exposition, tying men to the bare words of that primer, or catechism. As soon after they forbid all praying, but for the words of the canon. Now what can any ingenuous man think the design of all this was, but to rob us of preaching and praying, and by this of the Gospel and true religion wholly in conclusion? Only to do it for fear of noise and tumult, to do it so as we should neither know nor see.

And for the abstractive way. The rebuilding of Rome, among us, they did not proceed by the same steps.

First, urging the constant and full practice of the old ceremonies beyond the intention either of law or canon. Then bringing in an idolatrous worship of new popish superstitions without warrant either of law or canon, but their own paper injunctions; forcing their observance on ministers and people; but by pauses and degrees.

First, the table must be railed in; soon after set in altar posture.

Then, all must be compelled to come and kneel before it, or not receive the sacrament.

Then it must be cried up as the *sanctum sanctorum*; the place of God's chief residence on earth; the seat and throne of God Almighty. And on this, all men's faces in prayer must be turned towards that. Men may, yea must say some, adore and bow before it.

What could the intent of all this be? But after the altar to bring in the sacrifice, and with their wooden worship, the God made of bread, only to do it by degrees, that we should not know nor see. So in doctrine. First, bring in Arminian doctrines, then the popish will easily follow. Let the serpent but wind in his head, he will soon work in his whole body. Let Arminianism but obtain countenance and license in the kingdom; our pulpits, schools, presses, will soon be filled with popish doctrines. Witness the publishing of so many points of popery one after another, especially those two. That the Pope is not antichrist. And that the Church of Rome is a true visible Church. *Alta sic surount mania Rome.* So (according to the rule of their master Jesuit) they seek to reestablish Rome by degrees. They said they shall not know nor see.

His second rule is this, to press the examples and practices of some as a good means to draw on the rest. And was this not familiar with them? To dazzle the eyes of the meaner and less judicious people of the kingdom, with the practices of great persons. If any begun to startle, or be troubled at the matter, what was their present answer? My Lord Bishop does so and so. And my Lord's grace of Canterbury does so and so. The knights of the most noble order of the garter bow, versus Altair, towards the altar at their installment. His majesty's chapel is so and so adjourned. By these and the like pretenses casting a mist before the people's eyes that some did not have, and others dare not see anything tending towards the altering of religion. Our adversaries said, "They shall neither know nor see."

His third rule is this, that arch-heretics and such as are teachers of heresy must be banished from the Commonwealth, at once if it may safely be done, but if not, by degrees. It is easy to know who are the Jesuits, arch-heretics, and the most active orthodox Protestants. For the rooting out of such, the Jesuit prescribes a method of twelve or thirteen steps. For which (though well worth the relating) prefer you to his book, lest the discourse should swell too much. Only in sum, let me show you how their operation has been according to this rule. The arch-heretics and teachers of heresy in England have been counted the *puritan preachers*, though they teach nothing but that which is consonant to Scripture, and the public doctrine of the Church, yet they are the *teachers of heresy*. And being too many to root out at once, it must be done by degrees, that it may be effected with more ease, and less noise.

First, cast all those out of the ministry that will not be punctual and full conformists to the old ceremonies. Next (because there were a company of conformable puritans as themselves styled them) they procure an edict for recreations on the Lord's day, and this must be published by ministers; that such as could stand under the ceremonies (though groaning for the burden) might fall and be broken in pieces under this. And yet because some men suspected of Puritanism might have a latitude here beyond their brethren; they have a third engine, and that is enjoining new ceremonies and adorations, that if any could swallow the book, yet they might discover and cast them out by straining here. To this they add a fourth, prayers and proclamations to be read against our brethren, the Scots. And the last and greatest engine, which was like the powder plot against the godly ministry of the nation, to blow up the relics of them at once, was the oath for Episcopacy. By these successive stratagems they made account utterly to extirpate those arch-heretics.

As it was sometimes said to Elijah, "Him that escapeth the sword of Hazael shall Jehu slay. And him that escapeth the sword of Jehu shall Elisha slay," (1 Kings 13). So had they said, "Him that escapeth the dint of the ceremonies shall the book of sports slay, and him that escapeth the book of sports shall the new injunctions slay. And him that escapeth the new injuctions shall the proclamations slay, and him that escapeth the proclamations, shall the earth slay," and all this by degrees and pauses that they shall neither know nor see until we slay them and cause the work to cease.

The fourth rule is this, that those which are adversaries to the true religion (which with him is popery) be put by their dignities, places, and offices. I think none here is such a stranger in England but from his own knowledge can witness this. The bestowing of all offices, the collating of benefices, the election of masters, and fellows of colleges in both universities, who had the overruling hand in them all, the power of mandamus; but Canterbury and his faction? And whom were they conferred on usually? Men infamous for and impudent in Arminian and popish opinions? (We must protest Arminianism and bold faced popery as the only speedy unerring way to Church preferment.)

His fifth rule is to make the Protestant religion odious, by laying load on such tenants as are most subject to harshest constructions. In this our adversaries have not been sparing. *Quos plaustra convitorum*, have they poured out on some doctrines of our religion, especially the point of grace? The pulpits of Italy and Rome, never spit more gall and venom against the doctrine of election, free grace, justification by faith, perseverance, no never sweat more to exaggerate seeming absurdities, which carnal men would draw from them than some of ours have done.

His sixth rule is to ferment the quarrels that are among the Protestants and strengthen that party that is nearest to prescribe one thing as the proper means of England's cure. For who (he says) might not easily reduce the puritans of England into order, (you know what the Jesuits reducing into order is) if he could extort from them, an approbation of the Bishops? And had they not tempted and almost effected this? They had made us their slaves before, and were they not about to make us swear we would be so forever? Certainly though nothing but episcopacy in the surface of that oath, yet popery was in the thrall of reducing the puritans of England into order, *sensu pontificio.*[12]

---

[12] So Leonitus Bishop of Antioch a disassembling concealed Arian was observed to disrespect all orthodox men and prefer no one in the church but such as incline to Ariniam (*cf.* Theod. 2.24).

His seventh is this, that all private conventicles and public meetings must be forbidden. For private conventicles, you all know that to meet together to pray or to confer (which with them was a conventicle) was *Peccatum irremissible*. A man might at a better rate almost answer anything then such a meeting.

For public meetings. The ancient laudable exercising of prophesying (I mean not in that sense the word is lately taken for private spirits to interpret Scripture, but prophesying by men in office peculiarly gifted and called to that work) these are banished. The public and most frequented lectures blasted (which had of long time been used in many parts of the kingdom) had become peculiar. A sermon was next to the Church, the forbidden fruit, when they had none as some or worse than none. Our adversaries have been but too diligent to suppress not only private conventicles, but public assemblies.

The eighth means is by severity of laws and punishments to compel the obstinate unto duty and yet rigor of the law must be slowly drawn out and not against all, but only such as are most dangerous. Now what severity, not only *Ad summum jus* to the highest jot of the law, but even *supra jus*, beyond the extent and rigor of the law, has been used to such as stood in the way of their great design, let the walls of the high commission speak. Our chronicles report that when our forefathers demolished the abbeys, they found in their walls and vaults and ponds heaps of skulls and bones, the monuments of their smothered cruelties. I doubt not but the abolishers of that high commission have found as manifest evidence of their cruel practices. Heaps of the blood of innocents, (Micah 3) whose skin has been shed from off them, and their bones broken, and they and their families chopped in pieces as meat for the cauldron. And this fruit they reaped of their severity, managed with this art which the Jesuit promised. That though compulsory reformation could do no good on old standers, yet it would render the younger sort of Catholics.

The ninth means and (as he says) of all the rest most effectual is, that such as are in authority religiously practice and maintain integrity of life and purity of manners. The reformation of religion (that is the introducing of popery into a reformed Church) will go on very slowly and prove very difficult unless the prelates and doctors shall outshine the whole Commonwealth, not only in innocence, but in reputation and of integrity.

And certainly this rule they had conned (some of them) *ad mussim* or else they could never have obtained so far on the heart of our sovereign as to leave the disposing of all Church affairs wholly unto them. If they did not have in his eye, demeaned themselves as the only saints on earth as incarnate angels, men wholly composed of devotion to God, compassion to his Church, grief for the rents and breaches of it, zeal for the peace and good of it. What but that should prevail with our sovereign, to abandon this Church into the hands of that faction, I do not know. But undoubtedly it stands not with reason, that a Protestant prince should knowingly and willingly give way to the reestablishing of the popish religion, and in this *ipso facto*, divest himself of his supremacy, and lay his head at the Pope's feet, for him to kick off the crown from his royal brow, with a spurn of his disdainful foot at pleasure. But why the Bishops (especially such of them have been observed to wish well to popery) should contrive and carry on such a plot, some reason may appear. Nor could they once have obtained this; that popery should have triumphed over the reformed religion. The miter would soon have trampled on the crown. *Hac evim est veritas,* Belarmine says, This is the truth, whatever custom has introduced that the Bishop is the father, and Pastor, and Doctor, as well of the prince, as of the rest of the people. And according to these appellations, the prince ought to be subject to his Bishop, and not the Bishop to his prince. *Unusquisque* says Suarez, Every King is subject to his Bishop in *spiritualibus,* unless he is exempted by the Pope. A brave world this had been for the prelacy, and the whole clergy too, to have been exempted from the power of laws, and civil judicature *Leges non obligant*, says Suarez again, The law does not bind the clergy, by virtue of any lack of jurisdiction, neither can the King bind the clergy, by laying any special law on them. And again Ecclesiastical persons are privileged in court, not only in the case of ecclesiastical, but of civil crimes. An immunity which a corrupt clergy would be glad of.

And therefore, though there can be no reason conceived why a prince professing the protestant religion, should decline to popery. Yet you see there is reason why a proud prelacy, and a corrupt clergy should underhandedly endeavor to bring it in. And you see the method and ways by which they may compass their designs, and neither prince nor people know nor see. These were their practices for many late years, as you all know, let any ingenuous spirit judge of their intentions. I have only let you see from whose quiver they have drawn their shafts; judge by that of the mark to which they aimed. You have seen whose heifer it is that they plowed with; judge by that of the seed they would have sown. If they never knew that a Jesuit had delivered these rules for the altering of religion in a Christian state, they were very unhappy in complying so exactly with them, when they did not know them. And what can we think but that they were acted by the same genius, or the same *angelus informans*, that the Jesuit was, when he penned them. But if they did know (as it is most probable they did) that these were the rules, thus the art delivered by a Jesuit for the subverting the true reformed religion, and the introduction of popery again, and yet knowingly and *de industria* conform to them and made proof of them, what can we think was their intention but to alter our religion. They had said, "they shall not know nor see, till we are in the midst of them, and cause that work to cease."

But blessed be the Lord, who has not given us up as a prey to their teeth. Blessed be the Lord, that by the hand of this Parliament has frustrated the plot. We all hope, forever.

But did I say forever? May we hope it? What? Are our adversaries all destroyed? Or have they left off plotting? Neither, and yet I hope we may say forever, "This great plot of altering religion, prevented forever." As for our adversaries, verily, if ever they strained their wits to exceed themselves in plotting mischief, it has been since this Parliament. Such a succenturiation there has been of plots that we may say of them, as she of God, "A troop cometh." Many of them indeed have proved abortive, miscarried before they came to a growth capable of full discovery, and so are more easily denied than proved. Besides some ridiculous things have been sent forth into the public of purpose to outface the truth, and fully the glory of our deliverances from many and real dangers, which possibly may be the reason why some men are so incredulous, they can see no adversaries, they apprehend no dangers, the Parliament needs no guard; there is no necessity of settling the militia of the kingdom, if there is any such here, and you that are men of reason hearken a little.

First, do you not think that there are as many papists in England now, as there were at the time of the Powder Treason? I do not know how there should be fewer, but more; unless the preaching of popish doctrines, complying with popish ceremonies, setting up public masses, tolerating a convent of friars, relaxing the laws against popish priests is a means to convert papists, there cannot be fewer than was at the time of the *Powder Treason*.

Secondly, consider whether the papists have any better doctrines, dispositions, principles now, than they had then. Their faith was then faction, their religion rebellion, in the judgment of the state who spoke as they found. Have they since changed their faith, altered their religion, that our state should alter their judgment of them? Do they not yet hold it, as lawful as meritorious to promote the Catholic cause, *vi vel fraude*, by violence or treason, now as they did then? Have they retracted that doctrine of theirs; that kings and princes which are not Roman Catholic may be lawfully killed by any private person, and that the killing of them is a generous, virtuous heroic exploit? To be compared with the greatest and most praise worthy actions? A most holy, worthy, commendable, praiseful work? Those that conspire against the life of such Kings and Princes are magnanimous persons. Their courage is more than human, heroic, divine. Their punishments are true martyrdom, they shall receive reward in the kingdom of heaven.

Have they yet revoked the assertion? It is necessary in any case that religion be maintained even with the death of kings. Or that of the Jesuits Varidus to Barrius; that there could not be a more meritorious work, than for him to kill the King. Do they not to this day honor Garnet, that arch powder traitor, as a saint? Have not their late writers crowned him with fresh encomia sticks? And does our state not have reason to have a watchful and prudent jealousy over men informed with such desperate principles, and thus encouraged to all bloody designs? Especially such of them as are Jesuits and seminaries, of whom we may truly say as Amilcher did of his sons, he bred them *Tanquam Iconinos catulos in pernitiem Romani imperij*; as lions whelps for the destruction of the Roman empire. So do they breed their novices, as lions whelps for the destruction of the English Church and kingdom. And as Hannibal when he was only nine years old, swore on the altar of their gods, "That as soon as he was able he would be a deadly enemy to the people of Rome." So did they in effect swear as much against us: "I will help to defend and maintain the Roman papacy against every man. Heretics and schismatics, and all such as shall rebel against our Lord, the Pope, and all his successors, I will persecute and oppose." The whole *Frie* of them are *conjurati hostes Ecclesia & Reipublice.* They declared themselves so in the Powder Treason. And as long as they retain their old religion, they cannot but retain their old disposition.

Thirdly, there being papists among us now as there was at the time of the powder treason. They being infected with as bloody doctrines and principles now as then.

Consider thirdly, whether they may not pretend to themselves as just causes to put them on all bloody and desperate designs now as they did then. Were they crossed in their designs of a toleration of their religion then? Their expectations were raised higher now. They hoped for a revolting to their religion, and are crossed in that. Did they fear the state would make some further provision for the suppressing of popery then? And did they not fear the state would make some farther provision for the further extirpation of it now? Were they so enraged then? Surely they are mad and desperate now. Were their thoughts so full of blood then? Surely they are full of hell now. And of a truth, if there had not been one plot nor treason discovered all this Parliament's time; yet there is good reason why the Parliament should on these considerations arm the kingdom for its defense. (And the whole nation is bound to them for their care in this) to prevent our adversaries, lest they should say, "We will come on them, and they shall neither know nor see, till we are in the midst of them, and slay them, and cause the work to cease."

But what need these Ambages? When the bloody monsters of Ireland speak out and tell all the world, the war they have kindled is against the puritan Parliament of England. So that *ex professo* there has been treason against this Parliament, and our adversaries have said (varying the words of the text a little), "We will come on them, though they know and see it, and slay them, and cause the work to cease."

And, O that Ireland had been guilty alone! That England, England had not been conscious of such treacherous practices. But it is too apparent now, that even in England, in the midst of us, in our bosoms have been the most dangerous, and desperate practices against our peace and religion that ever yet were known. Let me not seem to detract from the glory of that great deliverance, if I say, they do exceed the *Powder Treason*. Those traitors laid theirs (which every true, loyal heart bleeds to think of) in the bosom of our sovereign. They covered their treason with earth, these with heaven. With pretenses of defending the Protestant profession, the prerogative of the King, the laws and liberties of the land, by which they have not only captivated many of the injudicious multitude; but even the throne itself, "The breath of our nostrils, the Anointed of the Lord is taken in their pits; of whom we said, under his shadow we shall live," (Lamentations 4:20). Their pretenses have so far prevailed with our sovereign, that he confides more in a popish party than in a Protestant Parliament, "This is a lamentation, and must be for a lamentation," (Ezekiel 19:4). They now pretend to be all for the King, the King, as much as the Jews for Caesar, "We have no King but Caesar. No King but Caesar," (John 19:15). As if Caesar had no such loyal subjects in the world as the Jews were. But when they had served themselves of Caesar and abused his power to the murdering of Christ, they soon discovered themselves. And Caesar had no such desperate rebels, and implacable enemies on earth as they were. So the papists and their faction cry out, the prerogative, the King and Caesar. As if the King had no such subjects and friends on earth as they are. But mark my words, if ever they can serve themselves of his majesty. And by the abuse of his power have their wills, to murder Christ in his members and root out the Gospel and the professors of it (which Lord in mercy preserve his majesty from) but if they once obtain this, if they do not prove the most deadly and desperate enemies his master ever had, let me die the death of a false prophet.

The searcher of hearts knows (O that Sovereign knew so well) how the hearts of all his loyal Protestant subjects bleed within them for the foul of our Sovereign. To see his confidence removed from his true protestant subjects, whom he can only confide in, and whom Catholic princes trust rather than those of their own religion. To see, I say, his confidences withdrawn from them, and leaning on a company of popish, bloody wretches, whom no Protestant prince but himself ever did trust, "Lord give thy judgments to the King." Does his majesty not know that with the papists all Protestants are heretics. And with heretic Kings and Princes they take a short course, have a quick way of dispatch? Does his majesty not know, or will none of his great divines inform him, that the Catholic doctors, hold it lawful for any private person to kill a heretic King? Yes and that though he is not sentenced, excommunicated, or deposed by the Pope, if his heresy is notorious *Cajetan.* Or if he is publicly defamed for a heretic. Or so reputed by grave and judicious men. No, that it is not only lawful, but necessary. Not only that they may do it, but they are bound to do it. And that by the command of God on peril of their souls. And this is not a private opinion, but the opinion of all their divines, and of their whole Church, if we may believe them. Nay, it is not only lawful and necessary, but if people should be loathe to offer violence to their Prince, the Pope may command and compel them to it.

When the papists shall as publicly and unanimously disclaim this doctrine, as they have proclaimed it, and the Parliament broach such doctrines and the Protestants drink them in. Then let his majesty die from his Parliament, and Protestant subjects to secure his life and crown among the papists. But in the meantime, O what a piece of arch-treason was it! By sowing contention between his majesty and Parliament to draw his majesty to betray himself into the hands of a generation, that in conscience think they may kill him when they please.

None are taught that in conscience they are bound to kill him, if he does not please them in matters of religion and may with a nod from Rome be commanded to kill him. O what an inextricable labyrinth these wretches have brought our Prince into, by persuading him, the intentions of his Parliament are against his dignity and prerogative? The Lord rebuke those that so persuade him. Yes the Lord rebuke you, Satan. But what better suggestions can breathe from those that are Parliament adversaries from generation to generation. This is what has moved his majesty to cast himself into the arms of papists. Where he is as safe as a lamb in the midst of wolves. Suppose a party (pretending his prerogative, and by this seducing a great part of the kingdom to assist them), suppose they prevail. What a condition is his majesty in? Either he is in danger of losing his religion, and being reconciled to Rome, or if not, of losing his life, and forfeiting his crown from himself and his posterity. No possibly he may lose all, though he should abandon his religion and be reconciled to Rome. For so Simanca determines, "If Kings or other Christian Princes be turned heretics, their subjects are presently freed from their dominion, neither shall they recover their right again, though they may be afterwards reconciled to the Church. And as a King loses his kingdom by heresy, so his children lost their right of succession." And to look no farther than Henry IV of France, did his being reconciled to Rome secure either his life or crown? Lord give your judgments to the King, Lord give your judgments to the King.

I do not fear of this. The papists have taken the oaths of supremacy and allegiance. And what are we the better? An oath on the conscience of a papist is like a collar on an ape's neck. That he will slip on for his master's pleasure, and slip off again for his own. Hear but how Pascenius scoffs at King James for the invention of that oath, and you will see his son has little cause to trust them for all their taking it, "See," says he, "how simple they are in all their craft; he thought he had composed an oath with so many particular circumstances, that it could not with a safe conscience be dispensed with. But he could not see that if the Pope loosed the oath, all the knots of it whether concerning allegiance to the King, or not suffering the oath to be dispensed with, they are all united. Yes, that which is more admirable. If the oath is publicly declared to be unjust, it binds none, but *ipso facto* as made void. Now the Pope has sufficiently declared this oath of the King's to be unjust, so that the obligation of it vanishes into smoke and that bond, which those wise men thought to be as strong as brass is less than a straw. And now what faith does his majesty give to, or what confidence can his majesty have in the oath of these men.

And yet as if it were not enough. To withdraw the heart of our sovereign from confiding in his subjects, the venom of this treason reaches farther. And as Achitophel knowing that if Absalom were reconciled to his father again, it would be his destruction, put Absalom on such a business as he knew was scarcely capable of reconciliation, (2 Samuel 16:23). So this cursed faction knowing that on union between his majesty and Parliament follows their deserved ruin. Have counseled, yea even compelled his majesty to that, which (if anything) might make the breach between his majesty and his subjects incurable. O that vast effusion of English blood which has already not only in Ireland but in England! The sun has not seen so many carcasses of English men lying on their native soil in many hundred years. The LORD see and avenge it on them that are the original cause of this bloodshed. The violence that is done to me and my flesh be on you, O papacy, shall the inhabitant of Ireland say. And my blood on you, O prelacy, shall England say. This the Helena for whose sake all these wars are. For the defense of the prelacy the Scotch War was commenced (though prerogative and monarchy was pretended) and for the same we may conceive the war of England if pursued. We may say to that faction as Joab did to David, "Thou regardest neither Prince nor servants, for this day I perceive that if Absalom had lived and all we had died, it had please thee well," (2 Samuel 19:6). They regard neither Prince nor people, for we may easily perceive that if England and Scotland imbrue themselves in one another's blood, or England tear out its own bowels, though we all die, so the hierarchy survive, they would be well pleased. "Shall they escape by their iniquity? Thou Lord in thy displeasure shall cast them down."

As for our Sovereign, you O God in whose hands the hearts of Kings are, free his heart from the counsels and engagements of mischievous men and men of blood. Give him a true understanding of and a due confidence in the loyal affections of his Protestant subjects. Bring him back among us rather in the prayers and tears than in the blood of his people.

And you, my brethren, so many as have any spark of loyalty in your breasts, and I hope you are full of it, desire and seek the same thing, you of this city. You of the honorable nation of the Scots, do not be the last to bring the King back to his house, you are his brethren, you are his bone and his flesh, why should you be the last in bringing the King back to his house again? Even to his house of Parliament? Assuredly if his majesty's life were bound up in one hair of his head, as

Nisus was, he might be more secure there, then he can be amongst papist and cavaliers, if every hair of his head were a life.

I come to a few words of *exhortation*. First to you, the members of the honorable house of Parliament. Secondly, to you, the rest of my brethren. First, for you honorable and beloved. This text, this truth tells you what you must look to meet with. God has opened to you a great door of opportunity for the promoting of his Church's good, but there are many adversaries. God has called you together to a great work, but you must look our adversaries; for they will do their utmost either by craft or cruelty to cause the work to cease. That which our Savior spoke to his disciples to confirm their hearts against the persecution of their adversaries. The same I say to you, steel your hearts against the oppositions of your adversaries. So says our Savior, they persecuted the prophets that were before you, the same I say to you, (Matthew 5).They so maligned the Parliaments that were before you. They so slandered the Parliaments that were before you. They so plotted against the Parliaments that were before you. So they said of them, "We will come on them, and they shall neither know nor see, till we are in the midst of them, and slay them and cause the work to cease." Therefore, be terrified of your adversaries in nothing. *Durate & vosmet rebus servate secundis.* Bear up against their oppositions. After, ages shall keep thanksgiving days for your deliverance, as you now do for the deliverance of your forefathers. You have the remembrance of that great deliverance as an encouragement to your hearts this day *Qui custodivie Patres, custodiet etiam filios.* Deliverances past are the pledges of future deliverances. And this advantage you have about your forefathers. That whereas they knew neither their danger nor sought deliverance, yet were they delivered. You see your danger, flee to God by prayers, tears, fastings for deliverance. You have the prayers and tears of all the Churches and saints of Christ posting incessantly to heaven on the same embassage. And can you fail of deliverance? Remember again the goodness and greatness of your cause, and what Luther said to Melancthon. When on that opposition, which the German reformation met with it, he was much troubled and disquieted in his spirit, not for his own sake, Luther gives him counsel. That seeing the business was not man's but Almighty God's, laying aside all care, he would cast the whole weight of it on him. Why (he says) do you vex yourself? If God has bestowed his Son on us, why are we afraid? What do we tremble at? Why are we distracted, saddened? Is Satan stronger than him? Why do we fear the world which Christ has conquered? If we defend an evil cause, why do we not change our purpose? If the cause is holy and just, why do we not trust God's promises? Certainly there is nothing beside our lives that Satan can snatch from us. And though we die,

Christ lives and reigns forever, under whose tuition the truth is. We are indeed sinners more ways than one, but our sins shall never make Christ (whose cause we are engaged it) a liar. Let the Kings of the earth and the people rage as much as they will. He that sits in heaven shall laugh them to scorn. God has hitherto ruled and defended this cause without your counsels, above your counsels by naked and immediate providences has carried on his work in your hands hitherto, and he will give it the desired and prayed for issue, you may be confident of it.

Only as your cause is good, so see that your ways be good, remember what the Holy Spirit says, "When a man's ways please God, he maketh his very enemies to be at peace with him," (Proverbs 16:7). Let your personal ways, your public ways, what you act as men, what you act as Parliament men, please God. And reap the fruit of it in peace with, or triumph over all your enemies, for your personal ways, your conversations as men. O I think if any of you when you come to this assembly were of vain conversations (as other men are) yet so many prayers, so many sermons, so many fast days, so many dangers, so many deliverances, such variety of admirable astonishing providences, as you have known. Should have prevailed with your hearts to abandon all, and become eminently gracious, exact in all your ways. But if not, if there is yet any sin found on any of you, if any of you are conscious that any of his ways, though never so secret, are displeasing to God. Let me in the fear of God and in the bowels of our Lord Jesus beseech you, as you desire success either to your counsels or arms. As you tender the good of your native country (which I know is dear unto you, why else should you put your lives in your hands to do it service?) O break off your sins by repentance. Why should men of brace and honorable spirits, stain and diminish their glory by any one sin? That as it was said of Naaman, he was a mighty man of valor, but a leper, so are any of you? He is a prudent man, a brave speaker, but a profound statist, a worthy patriot, but O let there be no *but*, for God's sake, may you all be as the sun, without one spot. Why should a man denude himself of the protection of the Almighty for one sin? It was said of Achillis, that he was *styge armatus*. But he that repents of his sins, that believes in Christ, whose ways please God, is *Calo Christo, Deo armatus*, armed with heaven, with Christ, with God. Would any at such a time as this, in such a service as yours, be without this armor? O let your ways please God, and you shall not need fear your adversaries.

And as your personal ways, so your public ways. The things that you transact as public persons, let them be exact, walk and work by rule. Appolles being asked why he used such exact care in drawing pictures made this answer; *Pingo aternitati, I draw for eternity.* The things that you have now do to, are not only for the present, but future ages. Your actions will live in the memory of men as long as men shall live on the earth. You work for eternity, therefore be exact, work by rule, by line and plummer. Let all your aims be pure and good. Fix your eye on God's glory *Quicquid agas, propter Deum agas.* Let that be your motto which was his. *Propter te domine. Propter te.* Aim at God in all. And walk with God in all, see the pillar of cloud and fire going before you.

I am not ignorant, that your taking up of arms is made a matter of dispute. Now no time for that. Only this I say, it is no more than other of the Churches of Christ have been driven to before you, the Scotch, the French, the high and low Dutch Churches. In Germany when the Protestant Princes and states were treating about a defensive league not only lawyers, but divines were called to give their counsel in the thing. Luther, who had always taught that the magistrates ought not to be resisted, and in the times of the Anabaptist tumults, had written a book to that purpose, being one in the consultation, and hearing the lawyers declare; that it was permitted by the fundamental law, sometimes to resist, and that now, matters were brought to that very state of which the laws made mention. Luther ingenuously professed that he did not know so much before. And because the Gospel does not impugn nor abolish national laws, because in such a time as that was; uncertain and full of fear, many things might fall out so as not only law but conscience and necessity might put arms into their hands. Therefore, he concluded that they might lawfully enter into a league of defense, whether Caesar himself, or any other in his name should make war on them, and presently published a book therein admonishing all men that they should not yield obedience to the magistrates, commanding them to that war against the league.

I know that many in the land charge the preachers of the kingdom, and those that have petitioned you so often for reformation in doctrine, worship, and discipline, as the kindlers and fomenters of this unnatural war; but, "O Lord if we have done this, if there is such iniquity in our hands, then let them tread down our life on the earth; and lay our honor in the dust. We have not desired this woeful day O Lord thou knowest it, our desire was to have obtained the establishment of religion in purity, and peace without blood, O Lord thou knowest it." *Quod si non aliter.*

But if the sins of England are such, and the engagements of our adversaries to their superstitious ways be such; that there is no other way to have popery cast out, the Church reformed, the Gospel assured to us and our posterity than this. *Hac mercede placet.* The will of the Lord be done. Go you on undauntedly in that blessed work of reformation.

Think you hear Christ speaking to you as Casar did to his ferrymen in a storm, *Perge contra tempestatem forti animo casarem fers and fortunam casaris.* Bear up courageously against the storm, you carry Caesar and Caesar's fortune. Think that you hear Christ saying this to you!

Pergite contra tempestatem forti animo Christum fertis and fortunam, ecclsiam, gloriam Christi. Bear up courageously against the storm; you carry Christ with you, and the Church the fortune, the glory of Christ. If the tempests and floods of the ungodly rise against you, remember you have not only the sighs and tears of God's people for you, but Christ embarked with you, who is able to rebuke the storms, and command a calm. You are a Parliament of prayers and tears, if ever any. And as Ambrose said to Austin's mother; *Non potest perire tantarum lachrimarum filius.* A child of so many prayers and tears cannot miscarry.

And yet as you are to be courageous, so to be confident. As to be confident, so vigilant. To have a watchful eye over, and a prudent care to suppress your adversaries. Darius the Persian, being enraged against the Athenians by a treachery of theirs, laid this injunction on one of his servants, that always as he sat at meat he should three times cry, *Here memento Atheniensium.* You need no such monitor. This fifth of November, as its yearly revolution cries loud in your ears,

Domini memento te papistarum. Not so much to enrage you against their persons, as against their religion. Not to say as he did there, *O Jupiter*. Lord, grant that I may be revenged on the Athenians, not to study revenge on the papists, so much as to suppress popery, if the one could be done without the other. What need is there of this, let a divine that had searched into the bowels of popery tell you. Papistry (he says) can neither stand with peace nor piety. The state therefore that would have these things, has just cause to suppress it.

But what course is to be taken for the suppressing of it? Shall we take that course for the suppressing of popery, which some of theirs prescribe for the suppressing of the truth. *Decretum fuit in consilius toletanis.* They made decrees in some of their counsels. That every King before he be installed should swear among other things, that he would permit no man to live in his kingdom, that is not a Roman Catholic, but will pursue all heretics with the sword. I know it is disputed among divines; whether it is lawful to use compulsory means in matters of religion. And no less among politicians, whether it would be successful. I shall neither take on me to determine those disputes, nor direct the wisdom of the great counsel of the kingdom in a course for suppressing popery. Only in brief, the means to be used to this end are, either sacred or civil. Acts of religion or of state.

For religious means, I conceive that the reestablishment of popery in Queen Mary's days was an act of state; and of the whole kingdom assembled in Parliament. So if the state, the Parliament now assembled would please to indict some day or days of solemn, national, professed humiliation for that sin of the nation, (which as far as I could ever learn, was never yet done) it might be a happy means to expiate that sin, and to purge the land from that blood of martyrs, which it yet groans under, and would blessedly prepare the heart of the nation for a more thorough perfect reformation. We observe it in particular persons that if they slide out of profane and sinful ways, into ways of more refinedness without any evidence of a sincere and proportionable humiliation. That reformation seldom proves lasting or saving. I do not know why the same may not be verified in national reformations. And among other things which possibly might be causes why the wrath of the Lord was not removed from Jerusalem, notwithstanding Josiah's so glorious reformation, this may be one, because the land was never humbled for the idolatries or bloodshed of Manasseh, but looked on the reformation as sufficient without humiliation, which verily has been England's course to this day. We have blessed ourselves in a kind of reformation. But never took to heart the idolatrous and bloody laws enacted by our forefathers, to be humbled for them.

Next to this, as a second means for the suppressing of popery, I would subjoin the casting out from among us of all appearances of popery; everything that looks like Rome, everything of which the papists may say, this you borrowed from us. It is true that the Israelites by God's express commandment, borrowed of the Egyptians' jewels of silver, and jewels of gold, but when they employed those Egyptian jewels to Egyptian worship, and turned their Egyptian gold into an Egyptian *god*, you know what followed. I do not condemn everything received from Rome, as simply evil. But certainly as long as the papists see any such thing among us in our public worship, they will but scorn us and our religion as imperfect and unable to furnish us in the service of our God without being beholden to them.

The means is to rid the Church of scandalous ministers, that what by their corrupt doctrine, by their abominable lives, have exceedingly hardened the papists against our religion and strengthened them in their own.

Fourthly, by complying as near as possible they may be like the other reformed Churches in all things. The resolution you have put on for uniting with the Church of Scotland is one of the most blessed things for the utter subversion of popery that has been since the first reformation.

And lastly, plant a faithful, painful, and powerful ministry through the kingdom. And give maintenance and encouragement answerable. But O Lord, in such a corrupt state of clergy and universities, where shall we find the faithful men to plant the nation with? The harvest is great, the laborers few, O pray to the Lord of the vineyard to send forth laborers into his harvest. To give the word that great may be the multitude of them that preach it.

As for civil means of rooting out popery, I shall wholly leave them to the counsel of the state.

Only one thing more let me add, which I cannot without sin forbear. If ever you would root out popery from England with the uttermost of your vigor, prosecute the affairs of Ireland, if popery prevails to the suppressing of the true religion there. Do not think you can prevail to suppress popery here. I know your domestic affairs are great, your occasions of expenses vast; yet I remember what the historian says of the Roman State. There was nothing that did more evidence the greatness of their spirits, than that as such a time, as Hannibal was even *Ad portus*. Their treasure exhausted by long wars. Their armies routed diverse times, the state at the lowest ebb that it ever was in. Yet even then, when a mighty war lay on their backs, they did not remit the care of any affairs, though never so remote from them. And nothing did more make Hannibal despair of taking Rome than what he heard, supplies of soldiers were sent out of the city into Spain, even then, when he with his whole army lay before their walls.

I do not know whether anything would more please God to procure a blessing on your affairs at home, I am sure scarcely anything would more daunt your adversaries at home and abroad, than to see you at such a time as this, sending supplies into Ireland.

And you my brethren, the rest of you that stand before the Lord this day. Do not withdraw your assistance from the honorable houses of parliament, in that or any other work so just, honorable and pious. You see they meet with opposition from their adversaries; it is impossible, it should be otherwise. O do not let them meet with discouragement from their friends, from their brethren. No question that it was worse to Nehemiah to hear Judah say, the strength of the bearers of burdens is decayed and there is so much rubbish, we cannot build the wall; than it was to hear the adversaries say, *we will come on them and they shall neither know nor see, till we are in the midst of them and slay them, and cause the work to cease.* That which the adversaries said was no more than he looked for. But this of Judah was unexpected. O do not let London say, and do not let England say, *The strength of the bearers of burdens is decayed. The expenses of the Irish war and of the English affairs are such a burden, we can bear no longer, our strength is decayed. We cannot build the wall. The work must cease.* I know your burdens this way have been great and in this city far greater than in other places of the kingdom, and are like to continue still. For though I hope it is not in the purposes of God to destroy England, nor to destroy London, yet I have though sometimes. The purpose and intent of God has been to humble, and attenuate London and England. For England's long continued peace had abundantly increased England's wealth, and the abundant increase of England's wealth had proportionately increased England's pride. The age before us did not know that excess of bravery in clothes and utensils that we were grown to. And the generation growing up was like to exceed us in both. God saw us labor so dangerously of a plethora as his wisdom and love judged it needful to abate and exhaust our fullness at least so much as is superfluous, and not matter of subsistence, but matter of pride to us, which if we can willingly and cheerfully resign to the disposal of God, we may possibly thereby obtain and secure our lives, law, religion, the things that are or should be dearest to us. But if we hug our wealth, when God would have us let it go, take heed that we do not lose that and all the rest. Methinks I read it in the footsteps of God towards England. God has said, "I will abate the wealth and pride of England." I think the succession of these three wars within these few years (which comes not without the special providence of that God who rules the kingdoms of men) the expenses of all which must lie on England, speaks it, that the purpose of God is to abate the pride and wealth of England. And methinks we should say as Mephibosheth did, "Yea let him take all, for as much as my Lord the King is returned again in peace to his own house," (2 Samuel 19:30). Might we but see our Sovereign Lord the King brought in peace again to his own house, and to his houses of Parliament. Might we but see the King of Kings on his holy hill of Zion, Christ in his beauty, on his throne, the Church reformed, truth and peace established. Let him take all.

I persuade myself every honest heart that is loyal to God, to the King, to the public and would willingly speak it and seal it, did not our adversaries by their crafty insinuations endeavor to divide as much between the Parliament and people as they have done between the King and Parliament. That would oblige us to persuade the people of this nation, with the ape in the emblem, to cut in two the arm of the tree on which they sit, and plunge themselves into a gulf and sea of misery.

To this purpose, as they have told his majesty, so now they tell the people that the Parliament will alter religion. A charge like that of Rabshakeh against Hezekiah and as true; when he would persuade the people God would not help them, because Hezekiah had altered religion, "If thou say to me, we trust in the Lord our God; is it not he whose altars and high places Hezekiah hath taken away, and said to Judah and Jerusalem you shall worship before this altar?" (Isaiah 36:7).

Truth is, this is all the alteration of religion, the Parliament has made: "They have taken away the high places and altars" that they have done and intended to proceed, to command all worship to be according to the rule of God's word. To say to England, you shall worship according to this rule, and this is the great crime of altering religion. My brethren, do not be deceived, as in natural, so in civil and moral things there is a double alteration. There is a perfective alteration, and there is a corruptive alteration, to alter religion so as to corrupt religion, was the plot and work of the popish prelates and their faction. To alter their alterations, to antiquate their innovations, to reduce religion to its pure original perfection (which cannot be done without alteration of something introduced) that was the purpose and work of the Parliament, and for this it is our adversary's cry against them, they will alter religion.

I but then the Parliament will alter the government of the kingdom. Yes, just as they altered religion. As in religion such alterations as tend *ad perfectionem* are not to be condemned. So likewise in policy and civil government Plato tells us, that in all commonwealths on just grounds there must be some changes. And that statesmen in this must behave themselves like skillful musicians, *Qui artem Musices non mutant, sed musices modum.*

244

But they do things without his majesty's consent. That is our grief and our adversary's triumph, that our adversaries have so far prevailed on the heart of our sovereign, as to persuade him to withdraw first his presence, then his assent from the great counsel of his Kingdom. And by this force them, either to do things without the consent of our sovereign, or else do nothing, but sit still, and expect their own and the kingdom's ruin. And in such a case, is it so high a crime to determine things necessary for the safety of King and kingdom, without consent of his majesty when it cannot be obtained? I have read that the Persian monarchs were accustomed to call the peers and presidents of their provinces to counsel. Every one of them had a plate or tile of gold to stand on in the council house, and if he gave counsel that the King thought well of, the plate of gold was given to him for a reward, but if he delivered anything contrary to the King's mind, *Flagrisca debater*. And one writer that Xerxes, in his expedition against Greece called his princes together, and spoke to them to this purpose; *least*, says he, I should seem to follow my own counsel, I have assembled you, and now do you remember; that it becomes you rather to obey, than advise. Our adversaries would fain have it so with the peers and Parliament of England, and have a long time been laboring to persuade his majesty it ought so to be, and would make the like impression on the people now. But you my brethren beware of their insinuations and know that those that divide between his majesty and Parliament, or between Parliament and people, are the greatest enemies of King, people, and Parliament. This is the first time ever that it was thought possible to draw the English nation to desert their Parliament, under the notion of adhering to their King. O let not this age bear the date of such infamy. Did Parliament ever do more for the laws and liberties of the nation with more danger and detriment to themselves? And will you when they have need of you leave them? Well here is our comfort, God has not left, God will not leave his cause, his work, his people, (1 Kings 8:57). The Lord our God be with us, as he was with our fathers. Let him not leave us, nor forsake us; that he may incline our hearts to him to walk in all his ways, and to keep his commandments and his statutes and his judgments. He, even he, maintains the cause of his servants, and of his people Israel at all times, as the matter shall require, that all the people of the earth may know that the Lord is God, and that there is none else.

THE DUTY OF SUCH AS WOULD WALK OF THE GOSPEL, TO ENDEAVOR UNION, NOT DIVISION NOR TOLERATION

Opened in a sermon at Paul's,
on the Lord's Day, February 8, 1646.

By Matthew Newcomen,
Preacher of the Gospel at Dedham in Essex

"Now I beseech you brethren, by the Name of our Lord Jesus
Christ, that ye ALL SPEAK the SAME thing, and that there be
no DIVISIONS among you. But that ye be perfectly joined
together in the SAME MIND and in the SAME JUDGMENT,"
(1 Corinthians 1:10).

LONDON.
Printed by *G.M.* for *Christopher Meredith*,
at the *Crane* in *Paul's Churchyard*,
1645.

INTRODUCTION

To the Right Honorable Thomas Adams, Lord Major of the City of London.

Right Honorable,

This sermon as it was first preached at your appointment, so at the same appointment of yours it is now published in print. It befell this sermon in its preaching, as it did Paul's, (Acts 13). Some contradicted, (verse 43) others were glad, and glorified the word of the Lord, (verse 48). To have your Lordship and the rest of your venerable colleagues in this latter rank of hearers, has been to me no small comfort against the censures of others. Though my chief comfort is this, the testimony of my conscience; that as of sincerity, that as of God and as in the sight of God, this sermon was preached to you, not as seeking to please men, but to edify the Church of Christ, and to contribute something towards the composing of our differences and closing of our breaches. If anything then communicated to the ear, and now offered to the view, may be successful in this kind, herein I rejoice and shall rejoice. God has called your Lordship to the government of this great city, and I do not doubt that you will find the divisions of this city, amongst the greatest difficulties of your government. We are at this time like men at sea, that have not only a tempest on them, but a commotion among them; not only the winds and waves raging furiously against the ship, but the mariners (who should do service in the storm) raging as furiously one against another. My Lord, the hand of providence has placed you at the helm of this city, he will give you wisdom, strength, and courage, to bring this ship (this city) safe out of this double tempest. Which is and shall be the prayer of him who is

Your servant in the Lord and in his work,

Matthew Newcomen

THE SERMON

"That ye stand fast in one spirit, with one mind," (Philippians 1:27).

Having formerly spoken of this place of the latter words of this verse, striving together for the faith of the Gospel. I shall at this time crave leave to lead you to the words immediately foregoing (in one spirit, with one mind) as containing matter of instruction, which if the Lord helps us to draw forth, may be both seasonable and profitable.

ἀκούω τὰ περὶ ὑμῶν, ὅτι στήκετε ἐν ἑνὶ πνεύματι, μιᾷ ψυχῇ συναθλοῦντες τῇ πίστει τοῦ εὐαγγελίου. Some join this with the former words (Μόνον ἀξίως τοῦ εὐαγγελίου τοῦ Χριστοῦ πολιτεύεσθε) and so read the sentence in this way, "That you stand fast in one spirit, with one mind." So the Syriac reads it this way; so Theophylact; so some Greek copies; and to that sense the vulgar translation is, *quia statis in uno spiritum unanimies.* Others refer the first part of this clause to the words foregoing, "That ye stand fast in one spirit;" the other to the words following, thus, "with one mind, striving together for the faith of the Gospel." So Beza, Zanchius, Elsius, and others.

By one spirit, here some understand the Spirit of God, which is One in itself, and One and the same in the hearts of all believers. So Beza, so Zanchius and Meelshurerus; therefore Zanchius reads it *per unum spiritum*, not *in uno spirita*.

Others make the words, πνεύματι and ψυχῇ synonymous, and by both understand the spirit or soul of man; and observe that usually (some say *always*) in Scripture, where these two, spirit and soul, or spirit and mind are joined together, they are both but one. Only the spirit is understood as the superior and rational part of the soul, the understanding. And by soul, the inferior and affection part; so that one spirit and one soul here, I conceive to be the same with one mind and one heart.

So that the thing which the apostle in these words commends to the special care and endeavor of the Philippians, it is *concord and union*. And this union it must be, first, a strict and close union; they are all to stand as firmly united together as if they had but one soul. Secondly, a sweet union, not forced on them, but naturally flowing from an inward uniting principle; one spirit and one soul. Thirdly, a holy union, it must be in and for the faith of the Gospel. Fourthly, a lasting, constant union, out of which they must never be shaken, they must stand fast in one spirit, with one mind.

DOCTRINE. The doctrine out of the words is this: that all those who would walk worthy of the Gospel, must endeavor a sweet, close, holy, lasting union among themselves.

I shall not need to go far to prove this. Be pleased to let your eye fall on the beginning of the next chapter, and you shall see the apostle with much vehemence pressing this very duty, "If there be therefore any consolation in Christ, if any comfort of love, if any fellowship of the Spirit, if any bowels of mercies, fulfill ye my joy, that ye be likeminded, having the same love, being of one accord, of one mind," (Philippians 2:1-2). As if the apostle had said, *If ever you tasted sweetness in Christ, if ever you found comfort in God's love, if you are Christians and have any fellowship of the Spirit, if you are men and have any bowels of mercies, if you pity me in my bonds, and would do anything to rejoice the heart of a poor prisoner of the Lord Jesus, fulfill my joy in this, that you be likeminded, having the same love, yes the same soul.*[13] A most powerful exhortation this is, in which the apostle heaps up not only words but arguments (*quot verba tot tonitrua;* as Hierome of another passage of Paul's epistles). One would think the apostle had said enough of this particular now, and that he need not speak one word more to these Philippians about this, yet he cannot think so. Therefore you have him again insisting

---

[13] *Vehemens quidem oratio, non verborum solum sed sententiarum etiam congeries abundans, & ad deliniendos permovendos animos plurinum valens.*

on the same thing, "Nevertheless, whereto we have already attained, let us walk by the same rule, let us mind the same thing," (Philippians 3:16). Beza conceives that the very rule which the apostle would have us walk by is this rule of union, *to mind the same thing*. No, the blessed apostle cannot content himself with this yet, but if there are only two in the Church of Philippi, and they but women that are at some difference, Paul cannot forbear but to exhort them by name, "I beseech Evodias and beseech Syntyche, that they be of the same mind in the Lord," (Philippians 4:2). These were two women in Philippi (so Theodore, Theopilus, Zanchius, and others) and it seems there was some breach, some dissension, either between the two of them, or between them and the rest of the Church. Zanchius brings many reasons to prove that it was in some point of faith and religion, in which that difference lay; and of this mind were Anselm, Primasius, and Remigius before him. Some would have looked on this so small a breach as a contemptible thing; what if a couple of weak women have taken up a singular opinion, need the great apostle trouble himself with that? But Paul knew how great a matter a little fire kindles, a dissension of two women may quickly divide a whole Church, therefore Paul pours water (or rather milk, which they say will quench wild fire) on this burning presently. I beseech Evodias, and I beseech Syntyche, *to be of one mind in the Lord*; as if to say, I would not have any one of you, no not one woman among you be of another mind from the rest of the people of God.

But was this not the apostle's peculiar and extraordinary care for the Philippians? And was it not a peculiar injunction on them? No, you shall find the like in other epistles, "Be of the same mind one towards another," (Romans 12:16). τὸ αὐτὸ εἰς ἀλλήλους φρονοῦντες. And see with what authority the apostle enjoins on them, "Now I beseech you, brethren, by the Name of our Lord Jesus Christ, that ye all speak the same thing, and that there be no divisions among you, but that ye be perfectly joined together in the same mind, and in the same judgment," (1 Corinthians 1:10). And again in 2 Corinthians 13:11, where the apostle is about to take his leave of the saints there, see what he leaves as his last advice with them, "Finally brethren, farewell, be perfect, be of good comfort, be of one mind, live in peace, and the God of peace shall be with you," (2 Corinthians 13:11). It is observable how the apostle makes this the *alpha* of his first epistle, and the *omega* of his last. The first duty he commends to the Corinthians in his first epistle is this union, and the last duty he commends to them in his last epistle is this union, as if this were the alpha and omega, *the primum and ultimum*, the beginning and perfection of Christianity, to be all of one mind.

So again, "I therefore the prisoner of the Lord, beseech ye that ye walk worthy of the vocation wherewith you are called, with all lowliness and meekness, with longsuffering, forbearing one another in love, endeavoring to keep the unity of the Spirit in the bond of peace," (Ephesians 4:1-3). See how affectionately, and with what a powerful heavenly *suada* the apostle here again presses this duty; I therefore such a one as Paul the aged, now in bonds, the prisoner of the Lord, ready to be offered up in the service of your faith. I therefore the prisoner of the Lord beseech you; though as your father in Christ, and as one that has been wrapped up into the third heaven, I might command you, yet I beseech you, I have only one request to make to you before I die, and it is this, that you walk worthy of the vocation wherewith you are called. God has called you out of darkness into his marvelous light, now let it be your care to walk worthy of this high, holy, and glorious calling. If you ask how you may do that, take this rule, "with all lowliness and meekness, endeavoring to keep the unity of the Spirit in the bond of peace:" where you have three things, *quid, quomodo, quibus medijs.* 1. The duty to be performed; 2. The manner of performing that duty; 3. The means by which they may be enabled to that duty. The duty is to keep the unity of the Spirit, "endeavoring to keep the unity of the Spirit." The word signifies no slight or slow endeavor, but an endeavor *full* of diligence and industry, endeavoring to keep. *Non jubes facere.* The apostle does not bid to make unity, but to have, not a perfunctory, but an exact care of that unity which Christ has made and wrought, that they neither trouble it, nor give any occasion for the disturbing of it, but rather with all care and diligence cut off occasions given by others, laboring with all their might to compose such differences as might arise, and performing with all their hearts all things that might tend to the preservation of unity. The manner how this duty is to be performed, or how this unity of the Spirit is to be kept is *in peace.* The apostle does not say, "keeping the unity of the Spirit in peace," but in the bond of peace, *ut significetur*, Hyperius says, that to the preserving of this unity, is required a solid peace among Christians, that cannot by any means be dissolved, *sed arctissme juncta moncat. Vbi onim pax decollat, ibi cesat unitas spiritus*, another says, "If this peace be cut off, farewell the unity of the Spirit." The means by which we may be enabled to perform this duty in this manner, to keep the unity of the Spirit in the bond of peace, are the graces commanded in the second verse, "with all lowliness of mind and meekness, with longsuffering, forbearing one another in love." And so full was the heart of this blessed apostle with zeal for this peace and union, that in the three following verses he prosecutes the same subject, and by seven arguments enforces this endeavor of union on them, of which more anon.

Nor was this Paul's zeal and care alone. You shall find the apostles of the same Spirit. So the apostle Peter, "Finally brethren, be ye all of one mind," (1 Peter 3:8), *omnes estate concords*. So Beza says, *unanimes*, so the Vulgate says the same, love as brethren. So the apostle John, in his first epistle, seems almost to be written on purpose to persuade to brotherly love, which is the root of union. Now if you add to these Scriptures, in which the apostles most industriously labor this in the hearts of the people by exhortation, those other Scriptures, where they do on behalf of the people endeavor this in heaven by prayer, that, "the God of peace and unity would work this unity and peace among them," you will see that this endeavor after union is a duty still of more worth and necessity. Of this kind is that of the apostle Paul, "Now the God of patience and consolation, grant you to be like-minded one towards another, (or to be of one mind among yourselves, *Ipsum sapere in alterutrum*, so the vulgar reads) according to Christ Jesus. That ye may with one mind and one mouth glorify God, even the Father of our Lord Jesus Christ," (Romans 15:5-6). But *instar omnium* is that of our Savior, (John 17) in that admirable, comfortable prayer which he there makes for his Church, see how often he lays in requests for this union, and presents this as his great suit to his Father, that his people may be one, "Holy Father, keep through thy own Name those whom thou hast given me, that they may be one as we are," (John 17:11). And again, "Neither pray I for those alone, but for them also which shall believe on me through their word; that they all may be one, as thou Father art in me, and I in thee, that they may also be in us, that the world may believe that thou hast sent me. And the glory which thou gavest me, I have given them, that they may be one as we are one, I in thee, and thou in me, that they may be made perfect in one, and that the world may know that thou hast sent me, and hast loved them as thou hast loved me," (John 17:20-22). (Where the word of comparison, (verse 22) shows *qualitatem*, not *aqualitatem unionis*.) Now, consider, if this union is such a thing, as not only the Spirit of God in the apostle Paul, but even the Son of God himself in the days of his flesh, made such earnest intercession for; is it not worthy of our endeavoring after? And that you may see that this holy sweet close union is not a mere *Idea platonica*, an imaginary perfection and blessedness, that ever was, nor never will be attained in this life; look but on the first and best times of the Church, and there behold the lovely face of this holy union. It is said, "they continued, with one accord in prayer and supplication," (Acts 1:14). And again, they continued, "*with one accord* in the temple, and breaking bread from house to house, did eat their meat with gladness and singleness of heart," (Acts 2:46). And again, "They were all *with one accord* in Solomon's porch. And again, "The multitude of them that believed, were of one heart and of one soul," (Acts 4:32). They had but one heart and one soul among them. But alas, my brethren, how may the Church of Christ take up the sad complaint of Job, "O that I were as in times past, as in the days when God preserved me, as I was in the days of my youth, when the secret of God was on my tabernacle." Now, you see there lacks neither precept, nor prayer, nor precedent in Scripture to commend to us the endeavor after a close, sweet, holy union, as our duty.

If you desire to know the particulars in which those that would walk worthy of the Gospel, are to endeavor a union among themselves; be pleased to review again the Scriptures brought for the proof of the point, and they will direct you in them.

I find some making mention of a threefold union or unity. *Unitas cordis, unitas oris, unitas operis*; a unity in heart, in word, in work.

First, in heart; you have this, "The multitude of believers were of one heart and of one soul," (Acts 4:22).[14] They were of one soul in regard of their judgment by unity in

---

[14] *Anima una quoadintellectum per unitatem fidei. Cor unum quoad affectum per unitatem charitatis.*

the faith. They were of one heart in regard of their affections by union of love.[15] By one heart and one soul, is meant an exact agreement both in doctrine and in will, says Beza; and subjoins, that in his ancient copy some words were added. Which Beza also found in several Greek copies, and translates, *non erat in illis separatio ulla*, there was no separation among them. *Nec fuit inter illos discrimen ullum*, there was no difference among them. Beza, *Nec erat inter illos controversia ulla*, there was no controversy among them. Happy men, and happy times, in this union of hearts that was among them.

This union of hearts is twofold, or implies two things; first, a unity of mind and judgment in matters of faith; secondly, a union of affection in love. Both which it is the duty of those that would walk worthy of the Gospel to endeavor after.

First, it is the duty of those that would walk worthy of the Gospel to endeavor after unity of judgment. Some observe that from my very text, in one spirit with one mind.[16] Paul admonishes the Philippians, not only of union of minds and wills, but of consent of doctrines and opinions, requiring mutual love, and the same mind. But this is very clearly and

[15] *Cordis & anima unius nominibus intelligitur summa tum in doctrina, tum in volunt atibus consensio.*

[16] *Philippenses non solum de animarum & voluntatum conjunctionis unitate, sed & de doctrina etiam & sententiarum consensione admonet, mutuam abillis charitatem, & eandem mentem efflagitans*

expressly required, "I beseech you, brethren, by the Name of our Lord Jesus Christ, that ye *all speak the same thing*, that there be no divisions among you, but that ye be perfectly joined together in the same mind and in the same judgment," (1 Corinthians 1:10). The word signifies a man's judgment, sentence, opinion in a matter, and is so used in this (1 Corinthians 7:25), where speaking of a case concerning virgins, "I give my judgment," or my opinion, says the apostle. And speaking of the widow, "she is happier if she so continue, after my judgment," (verse 40), or my *opinion*; so that when the apostle requires that they be perfectly joined together. *Consensionem requirit in eodem in religionis capitibus sensu*, says Beza on the place; he requires an agreement in the same sense, opinion, judgment, in the heads of religion. This is also intended in all those scriptures, where the apostle writes to the saints, to mind the same thing, or to be of one mind. So, (Philippians 2:2) which Beza translates, *unanimes, sententis uni*, agreeing and being one in your opinions. And in his annotations he says, *ad animorum (id est volutatum) conjunctione transit ad doctrina consensum, ut plena justique sit concordia*. The apostle passes from agreement in wills to agreement and consent in doctrine, that the agreement may be full and perfect. (So 2 Corinthians 13:11 and 1 Peter 3:8). All these call on Christians for oneness and sameness of mind, judgment, and opinion in the things of God in the doctrines of faith. And utterly condemn as sinful, that universal unlimited liberty of judgment and opinion, which in these times is so much contended for; for if it is lawful for every man to entertain and hold what opinion he pleases, how differing soever from the opinion and judgment of the rest of the Church and people of God, yet this is his opinion, and his judgment is persuaded of it, and he must follow his own judgment, and this liberty of judgment is (as some say) liberty of conscience, part of the liberty purchased by Jesus, and to restrain it, or set bounds to it, is in their language persecution, tyranny, *etc.* If this were true, sure Paul did very ill to charge the Corinthians with so much authority, to be of the same mind and of the same judgment. Might not some among the Corinthians have said to Paul, this is hard usage, this is to stretch a short man to the same length with a taller, and to cut a tall man to the same stature of one that is low? What, the same judgment? And the same mind? Will Paul not allow difference of lights and sights? Might not someone among the Corinthians have said, what if I am of the opinion that there is no resurrection, what has Paul or any man to do with that? It is my conscience, and it is my liberty, and what has any man to do with my conscience more than I with his? Might not Hymenaeus have said, *What if it is my opinion that the resurrection is past already, what has Paul to do with that?* Yes, Paul says, if you obstinately persist

I will excommunicate you, I will deliver you up to Satan, that you may learn not to blaspheme. Certainly this shelter, this asylum of error, falsely called liberty of conscience, was not thought of in former times.

But some may say, *what*? Are we so strictly tied, that one Christian may not differ from another in judgment or opinion? Is there no latitude? Must we all be of this same mind in everything?

I answer, you see it is that which the Spirit of God in Paul prayed for, which the Lord Jesus Christ himself prayed for, and therefore certainly it is that which we are to pray for and press after. And for any man to be of another mind than the rest of his brethren, the people of God are, as matter of humiliation, and not as matter of rejoicing.[17] It is that we should all desire, again and again we should desire it, that there might be a full agreement even in everyone of the least matters in the whole Church.[18] But seeing the issue does not answer our desire, it may be, our sins and our notorious ingratitude deserving the contrary, many will be of differing judgments. And indeed it can scarcely be but through the imperfection of our knowledge and corruption of our wills, there should be some differences of opinion and judgment

---

[17] *Optandum quidem nobis omnibus, iterum, iterum, optandum, ut in minimis quisusq, consensus firmus teneatur a tota Ecclesia*, says Aretius.

[18] *Sed cum eventus vetis non respondeat forte peccatis aliud promerentibus & insigni ingratitudine dissendentia judicia a multis proferenda esse.*

among us; but then it is that we should (not glory in, but) sigh under, as part of our imperfection cleaving to us while we are here on earth.

Question. But then the question will be, seeing there will be differences of judgment and opinion while we are on earth, then how or how far is this difference of judgment to be permitted? How, or in which may Christians differ from one another in judgment and yet ought to be tolerated and born with?

Answer. This is, my brethren, a very grave and difficult question, and to me, considering how many places there are in which the Holy Spirit calls on us to endeavor to be of one mind, of the same mind, and of the same judgment; it is easier to tell you, in which we may not differ in judgment, and in which differences in judgment may not be tolerated, than to tell you in which they may.

First therefore I say, that as an absolute unity in judgment, that we should all be of the same mind in all things, is scarcely to be attained in this life, though it is to be endeavored after; so a universal and absolute liberty of judgment for every man to differ when he pleases, and in what he pleases, to be of what opinion and faith he will, is not to be endeavored, if it might be attained, nor is it to be tolerated or permitted. I know no warrant, no pretense of warrant for it in all the book of God. Scripture nowhere says, "Let every man be of what opinion and of what faith he pleases, let every man be left to his own judgment."

"One man esteemeth one day above another: another esteemeth every day alike. Let every man be fully persuaded in his own mind," (Romans 14:5), if any man think these words of Paul patronize this opinion, it is but as they are mistranslated in the vulgar Latin, *Unusquisq, abundet sensu suo.* But there is no such thing in the text, and therefore Beza rejects it, and says plainly, *hac sentential Christiana esse non potest (this opinion cannot be Christian)*, as being in his apprehension contrary to that express Scripture, "Ye shall not do after all the things that you do here this day, every man that which is right in his own eyes," (Deuteronomy 12:8). And certainly this absolute liberty (or rather licentiousness) in opinion, which is so eagerly contended for by some, is not to be indulged to men.[19], "That same of liberty of believing anything is nothing else but a liberty of erring, and of erring in matters concerning the salvation of the soul, and an error there is most hurtful and dangerous; and therefore (he says) as it cannot be safe for sheep to be left to wander alone, through mountains and deserts, and graze where they please, lest they fall in on some unwholesome food, and poison themselves, or fall into the

---

[19] *Libertas illa quidvis credenda, nihil aliud quam libertas errand, quidem errandi in re anima salute concernente, in qua proinde error est longe nocentissimus & periculosisimus.*

paws of the wolf, and become a prey. And as it cannot be safe to leave a ship to itself, to be driven along before the wind, without any guidance or steerage. So neither can it be safe to leave a liberty to men to be of what faith or religion they list, or to hold what opinion they think good."

1. Particularly, liberty of opinion or judgment and tending to the blaspheming of his name and glory; as Judaism, Arianism, Socinianism. In the doctrine of the Trinity, and of the Lord Jesus, *Non licet luxuriari*. A wanton liberty of opinions and believing what men please is not to be born. If Hymenaeus and Alexander once come to blaspheme, away with them, cast them out, deliver them to Satan, (1 Timothy 1:20).

2. Nor secondly, is there such a liberty in such things as are pernicious and destructive to the souls of men; Such as are the main doctrines of popery, Arminianism, libertinism, "Though we, or an angel from heaven, preach any other Gospel unto you, then that which we have preached unto you, Let him be accursed. As I said before, so say I now again, if any (*whether man or angel*) preach any other Gospel to you then that what you have received, let him be *Anathema*,", "Notwithstanding, I have a few things against thee, because thou sufferest that woman, Jezebel, who calls herself a prophetess, to teach and seduce my servants to commit

fornication, and to eat things sacrificed unto idols," (Galatians 1:8-9, Revelation 2:20). So then here *toleration is abominable.*

3. Nor thirdly, is there liberty left in those things, in which our judgments and opinions in the discovery and practice of them will give just offense unto others, "Give none offense, neither to the Jews, nor to the Gentiles, nor to the Church of God," (1 Corinthians 10:32).

4. Nor fourthly, in such things, as in which the difference of judgment and opinion will necessarily and unavoidably, *ex natura rei*, produce a rent and schism in the Church of Christ, "Now I beseech you, brethren, by the Name of our Lord Jesus Christ, that ye all speak the same thing, and that there be no divisions among you. But that ye be perfectly joined together in the same mind, and in the same judgment," (Romans 10:17). "I beseech you brethren, mark them that cause divisions and offenses among you, contrary to the doctrine that you have received, and..." What? Tolerate them? No, "avoid them. I would they were even cut off that trouble you," (Galatians 5:12). Nothing can be clearer than these Scriptures are against the toleration of all doctrines, and particularly of those that trouble, rend, divide the Church.

A grave and judicious divine (*Crodus*) delivers his judgment in this particular so, 1. Those that are open atheists are not to be born; 2. Nor are those that would bring in confusion; 3. Nor those that would abolish magistracy; 4. Nor those that move unnecessary war; 5. Nor those that maintain open sins; 6. Nor those that take away, deny, or call in question any articles of faith necessary to salvation. I doubt if it were well examined, many of those opinions that infest our times, would fall under some part or other of this sentence.

But, (to speak a little to the positive) if there is a latitude and a liberty of judgment left, it is first in such things as are not clearly and positively laid down in Scripture, and therefore are not of the fundamentals and essentials of faith and worship, for there is for these clear and undoubted light in Scripture.

Secondly, it is in things that are of private and single practice, and not of open converse, or Church fellowship and communion. Those cases of eating or not eating, discussed by the apostle, in his epistles to the Romans and to the Corinthians, in which the apostle shows, there might be a liberty or indulgence, and Christians ought to bear one with another, in holding or practicing thus or otherwise; They were points of personal and domestic practice.[20], "There were two cases in which it was lawful to at things offered to idols; one, if a man bought them in the shambles, and ate them privately in his own house, (verse 25). The other is in case he bid to a

---

[20] *Duas species propones Apostolus, in quibus vesci liceat idolathytis,* says Beza.

private feast by a heathen, (verse 27). But to do this openly and professedly, in the idol's temple was a detestable thing. And yet even in these things this liberty is not to be assumed, at least not to be practiced without much needed tenderness and circumspection.

First, care must be had of keeping those opinions in which we differ from others, private to ourselves; not troubling and perplexing the consciences of others with them. This is the injunction, "Hast thou faith? Have it to thyself before God," (Romans 14:22). The faith there spoken of is a particular persuasion, touching the free use of all creatures, and the liberty of all days. And this faith, this persuasion was according to the truth (as it is clear by the apostle, "hast thou faith?" have it to thyself before God.", "Do not say, I am fully persuaded of my liberty, and therefore I ought to profess it, and hold it out in my practice, whatever become of others; It is the truth of God, and I must hold it forth."[21] No, says the apostle, have it to yourself. And if a man who has a private opinion, *in remedia* must keep it to himself, though it is a truth, much more must those whose opinions are false and erroneous. Certainly there is scarcely any difference of judgment so small, and in itself considerable, but the divulging and propagating of it may prove very dangerous and

---

[21] *Ego fidem habeo libertatis, ergo debeo eam profiteri, & factis ostendere, quicduid sit de alijs.*

pernicious, and in the event intolerable. Suppose a man should be of this opinion, that it is unlawful to eat things strangled of blood. If such a man keeps his opinion to himself, and makes it a rule only to his own practice. Let him enjoy it, until he can be otherwise informed, and persuaded in his conscience. But if he will now go publish this opinion and entangle the consciences of others, and seek to draw disciples after him, and make a party, and cause division and dissension amongst the people of God; this is not to be tolerated; *Persona private,* says a learned divine, *diversum sentientes, si quiete vivant,* "Private persons of a differing judgment, if they live quietly, frequent the public assemblies of worship, and are not discerned to disturb the peace either of state or Church, by any secret underminings, are to be tolerated, in hope of their conversion, and for public peace's sake. But if these men shall begin to spread their errors in public, to inveigle and draw others to them, to beguile the simple, and so to trouble the public space, they are to be restrained," says he, speaking of the duty of the magistrate in this case. So then, that is the first caution. If men have private opinions, opinions of their own, that they cannot be of the same judgment with the rest of their brethren; let them keep them private. Let them be *domestica judicia,* as Tertullian calls them, let them keep home, and not be seen abroad, "Hast thou faith? Have it to thyself before God."

A second condition to be observed in case of difference in judgment and opinion is, that though we cannot be of the same mind and judgment with others, yet we do not judge or despise those that differ in judgment from us, (Romans 14:3). There was difference of judgment among the saints in Rome, some thought it was unlawful to eat all kinds of flesh, as it was to eat herbs, and were ready to think them a company of weak, simple people, that would make scruple of it; others thought it absolutely unlawful to eat flesh, and thought that none would do it but profane men, men of no conscience, and therefore were resolved that they would eat only herbs. Now, this is that which the apostle reproves, forbids, "Let not him that eateth despise him that eateth not, and let not him that eateth not judge him that eateth;" whatever our differences in judgment are, we must take heed of despising and condemning one another.

A third condition is, that even when we cannot be of one mind, we yet labor to be of one heart; though we do *dissentire*, yet we must not *discordare*; though we cannot attain unity of judgment, yet we must maintain unity of affection, which is the second part of that *unitas cordis*, that union of heart which the Gospel requires. This is it which is required of is, "Be kindly affectionate one towards another in love," (Romans 12:10). So, "love as brethren," (1 Peter 3:8); if it should so happen that you cannot in all things be of one mind, yet notwithstanding love as brethren, φιλάδελφοι, says the apostle, which Beza in his first edition translates (as the vulgar does) *veritatem sectantes incharitate*, "following the truth in love," (Ephesians 4:15). Which I conceive both the notation of the word, and the scope of the place, if you consider the verse going before, will bear. And so the text imports, that love must set bounds to all our inquiries after truth, and we may not, under pretense of seeking truth, transgress the laws of and rules of love. If we cannot meet in every point of truth, yet let us embrace in love. If there is any difference in judgment, yet let there not be distance in affection. Paul and Peter may differ, Jerome and Augustine, Moscopolus and Philelphus, and yet be friends still, love as brethren.

And surely had we walked according to these rules, our division in England had not been so sad, so fatal as they are this day. Had all that profess the Gospel in England made conscience to be of the same mind, and the same judgment with their brethren, and the rest of the Churches of Christ, as far as possible. And where they cannot, where there is a necessity of differing, had they made conscience to keep their differences from appearing in public, to have their private opinions and faith to themselves, and not entangle the weak with their doubtful disputations; forbearing to judge or despise those that are not of their opinion, loving them still as brethren, not censuring them as profane, antichristian, fighters against God, men that will fully shut their eyes against the light; had these things (I say) been attended to on all hands, our breaches had never been so great as now they are, nor should the lovers of truth and peace have had so much cause to lament them. But thus much of the first kind of union that is required in those that would walk worthy of the Gospel, *unitas cordis.*

The second kind of union or unity required is *unitas oris.* As the people of God should have but one soul, so they should have but one lip, as one faith, so one confession of faith, one expression of themselves in matters of faith. Therefore the Holy Spirit calls on us not only to think, but to speak the same things, "Now I beseech you, brethren, by the Name of our Lord Jesus Christ, that you all speak the same thing," (1 Corinthians 1:10). Not only think, but speak. So, "That ye may with one mind and one mouth glorify God," (Romans 15:6). The people of God should not only have one mind, but one mouth. It was a happy and peaceable age when the whole earth was but of one lip, one language; the confusion of tongues at Babel brought in a world of other confusions. It is a happy thing when all the people of God can content themselves with the same language and expressions in the things of God. That same mind, that affectation of new and strange language, has ever been found prejudicial to the

Church of God. Augustine says, "They which coin new phrases, and new terms, and new definitions of things, for the most part are forging some new doctrines. For they refuse to speak as others do, that they may seem to be wiser than others are. *Semper ex mutate temere phrase secuta est dogmatum mutation.* Change of phrases has always ushered in change of doctrines.[22] Those that will not be bound to any form of speaking, at length bring forth strange monsters of opinions." It is that which both 2 Peter 2:13 and Jude 16 make a peace of the character of the false teachers, "They speak great swelling words of vanity:" And it is this that Calvin observes of the Anabaptists and Libertines in his days, they spoke such strange and uncouth high-flown language, as could not be understood by others, scarcely if at all by themselves. Now we should take heed of this, and in the things of God, content ourselves with those phrases and expressions that are passant in the Church of God, and not affect novelties. The greatest heresies that ever troubled the Church of Christ, have come out of the womb of new phrases and expressions; which made Melancthon wish, "That we were able to utter those things that are good and profitable, not only in the same words, but in the same syllables, and in the same letters. I set my Amen to it. O that we could be of one mind, and one mouth, all speak

---

[22] *Et videmus eos quid ad nullam formam loquendi se alligant mirifica portnta doctrina gignere.*

the same thing. That is the second particular of union we are to endeavor after."[23]

A third particular of that union we are to endeavor after, is *unitas operis*, union in way and practice. This the Lord has promised as a blessing to his people, "I will give them one heart and one way, that they may fear me forever for their good, and the good of their children after them," (Jeremiah 32:39). And, "That they may all call on the Name of the Lord, and serve him with one consent," (Zephaniah 3:9). Now that which the Lord promises, we must pray for, and that which we pray for, we must endeavor after one way, "Nevertheless, whereto we have already attained, let us walk by the same rule, let us mind the same thing," (Philippians 3:16). That is, Anselm says, "Let us all have a care of this, that whereunto we have already attained, we mind the same thing by believing, and walk by the same rule of discipline, that is, right living, that no man out of novelty, or leaning to his own understanding, desert the common faith or rule of right living." So much the text clearly tells us, that those who cannot be of the same mind in all things, should yet walk by the same rule, so far as they have attained to agreement. Unity in practice is to be endeavored, as well as unity in judgment. And thus now you have the explication of the point, what that

---

[23] *Unitam possimus eadem qua bona & utilia sunt, non tantum issdem verbis, sed & isdem syllabis & literis efferre.*

union or unity is, which it is the duty of all those that would walk worthy of the Gospel are to endeavor after.

I might bring abundance of reason for the further confirmation of this point, but I will bring no other than what the Spirit of God uses to enforce this doctrine by, and I will but point at them neither.

First, (he says), "There is one body," (verse 4) of which you are all members, therefore, "be ye one," let there be, "no discord" among you.

Secondly, "There is one Spirit," (verse 3). Even as in the natural body there are not diverse spirits or souls, according to the diversity of members, but one Spirit that gives life and motion to every member, so is it in the body of Christ, there are not as many several spirits as members, but one Spirit, which is so in the whole body as he is in every member, and gives life and motion to every member, "For by one Spirit we are all baptized into one body," (1 Corinthians 12:13), "and we have access unto the Father by one Spirit," (Ephesians 2:18). And though there are more, "diversities of gifts, yet there is the same Spirit," (1 Corinthians 12:4). There is one Spirit, therefore be one; keep the unity of the Spirit in the bond of peace. This bond *cannot* be broken, this unity cannot be violated, without offense to this one Spirit.

Thirdly, "You are called in one hope of your calling," (verse 4). So many of you as are called by the Gospel, one and the same salvation, heaven, glory is promised to you, and so many of you as have obeyed this calling, you are all commanded to hope for this salvation and glory all of you, there you shall live sweetly and blessedly together forever; therefore your peace and union ought no more to be divided here, then your inheritance can be divided hereafter. It is a shame for them to quarrel and fall out *in via*, that must live forever *in patria*. Indeed if God had not called all of us to the hope of the same inheritance in light, but had called some to a better, others to a worse condition, given some a double portion as Joseph did Benjamin, or a party-colored coat above others, as Jacob did Joseph, there might be some pretense for strife and envying, something that might give occasion to a falling out by the way. God gives not to one believer more than another, but gives to all of them immortality, eternal life, immortal glory; the brotherhood, the inheritance, you are all called into one hope of your calling, therefore be one. O *si animis nostris insideret*, says Calvin, "O that we would consider that we are under this law; that the children of God may no more differ among themselves then the kingdom of heaven can be divided; O how wary would we be in preserving brotherly love, how would we tremble at contentions, if we considered as we ought, that they all estrange themselves from the kingdom of God, that divide themselves from their brethren.

But I do not know (he says) how it comes to pass, that we can securely boast ourselves to be the children of God, and yet forget brotherly love one to another. The children of God have all but one hope, one inheritance, therefore all be but one."

Fourthly, the Apostle says, "There is one Lord," (verse 3), even the Lord Jesus. You are not as the heathen, "that have many gods, and many Lords," but to you there is but, "one Lord Jesus Christ," (1 Corinthians 8:6), and you are all his servants. Therefore be one. It resounds to the disadvantage and dishonor of him who is your only Lord, if there is envying, divisions, strifes among you that are his servants, therefore be *one.*

Fifthly, there is, "one faith," (verse 3). Both one grace of faith, *qua*, by which you believe; and one doctrine of faith, *qua*, which is believed. For all the saints, by one and the same grace, believe in one and the same Christ. Not in one Christ before the law, in another under the law, in another after the law. Nor the Jews one way, the Gentiles that are converted another way.[24] Therefore all believers ought to the utmost to endeavor to keep the unity of the Spirit in the bond of peace. There is one faith, therefore be one.

Sixthly, there is, "one baptism," (verse 5). Christ has not instituted several, but one baptism. All are baptized with

---

[24] *Non aliter in oriente, aliter in meridie, aliter in occidente.*

water in one Name of one God, Father, Son, and Holy Spirit. The Jews converted have not one baptism, the Grecian another; the free one, the bond another; the rich one, the poor another; but as they are all one in Christ Jesus, so they are all by one baptism baptized into Christ. Your baptism is but one, therefore be one.

Seventhly, says the Apostle, there is one God and Father of all, therefore be one. If all believers call on one and the same God and Father, how dare they, how can they break the bond of brotherly love? To see brethren, the children of one father, live in rancor and malice one against another, is a displeasing sight to all, but O how wounding is it to the heart of their own Father? So it is to God, to see his children out of charity, at discord. There is one God and Father who is over all, and therefore able to punish the miscarriage of all, and in all, and therefore thoroughly acquainted with the miscarriages of all, and in you all, for you are all the temple of God, and one God dwells in you all.[25] Those that would divide the unity of the faithful, do as much as it were to divide God that dwells in them.

Here then you see a seven-fold argument which the Apostle uses for the enforcing of this duty of my doctrine. There is one body, of which you are all members, therefore be

---

[25] *Ergo quid fidelium scindant unitatem, proinde facia ac si unum Deum patrem in partes vellent scindere.*

you one. There is one Spirit of which you are all temples, therefore keep the unity of the Spirit: "Ye are called in one hope of your calling," therefore be of one heart: "There is one Lord, one faith, one baptism, one God and Father of all," therefore you be one, seeing you are one in all these particulars, there is abundant reason for you to be one among yourselves.

Look again into this fourth chapter to the Ephesians, you shall find another argument for this endeavor after unity, "He gave some Apostles and some Evangelists, and some Prophets, and some Pastors and Teachers, for the perfecting of the saints, for the work of the ministry, for the edifying of the body of Christ, till we all come in the unity of the faith," (Ephesians 4:12-13). The text shows clearly that one main end which Christ aimed at in all the officers which he has set in his Church, and the gifts bestowed on those officers, it was to bring his people to unity. Not only to faith and the knowledge of the Son of God, but to unity in the faith, and in the knowledge of the Son of God. The Apostle here supplies us with a weighty argument to persuade us to keep the unity of the Spirit, which is so precious and of such esteem with Christ *for the sake of it*, (among other things, he has instituted the ministry) and officers which he has given to his Church. But this may suffice for the explication and proof of the point. I now come to the *application*.

Use 1. This truth, "That it is the duty of all those that would walk worthy of the Gospel, to endeavor a sweet, close, holy, firm union, and to be one in judgment and opinion, one in heart and affection, to speak the same thing, walk by the same rule," may serve in the first place to justify that *solemn league and covenant* which we have all taken; (I am sure at least all should have taken) and which you, Right Honorable and beloved, lately have renewed, even in that branch of it, and in those particulars which some more cavil against. Namely that last branch of the first article, in which we engage ourselves to endeavor to bring the Churches of God in the three kingdoms to the nearest conjunction and uniformity, in religion, confession of faith, form of Church government, directory for worship and catechizing, that we and our posterity after us, may as brethren live in faith and love, and the Lord may delight to dwell in the midst of us. As also the second article, in which we swear in like manner without respect of persons to endeavor the extirpation of popery, prelacy, superstition, heresy, schism, profaneness, *etc.* That the Lord may be one, and his name one in three kingdoms. I wish there were none that a few years ago, would have thought they could never have blessed God enough for such a covenant, that now spurn and scorn it, even in, no for these very clauses. But I beseech you, what is there in any of these particulars, but what is a duty incumbent from God, on everyone that would walk worthy of the Gospel, as you have heard abundantly proved this day. You have sworn to endeavor the nearest conjunction and uniformity in religion. What is that but to endeavor to be of one heart and one soul, (Acts 4:32), to endeavor to be perfectly joined together, in the same mind, and in the same judgment, (1 Corinthians 1:10), you have sworn to endeavor the nearest conjunction in confession of faith, what is that but to endeavor, "all to speak the same thing?" (1 Corinthians 1:10), "and with one mouth to glorify God," (Romans 13:5). You have sworn the same in reference to one form of Church government, directory for worship and catechizing; what is this but to endeavor to walk by the same rule? (Philippians 3:13). You have sworn to endeavor to extirpate popery, prelacy, superstition, heresy, schism, profaneness. What is this but to endeavor that there be no divisions among you, but that you be perfectly joined together, (1 Corinthians 1:10). All this is but your duty. And the purpose and intent of all this is that the Lord may be one, and his name one in three kingdoms. And that we and our posterity after us may as brethren live in faith and love, and the Lord may delight to dwell in the midst of us, what is, if this is not a sweet, close, holy, firm union.

Question. If any shall demand, how does it appear that we should endeavor such a union of all the Churches in a nation, in three nations; we grant indeed, that the saints of a particular congregation ought to have one heart and one way, to be of one mind and of one judgment. But how do you prove that such a thing is to be attempted and endeavored in a nation. The Philippians, Ephesians, Corinthians, on whom the Apostle enjoins this unity, were Churches of a particular congregation.

Answer. This is *gratis dictum*, that the Churches of Ephesus, Corinth, Philippi, consisted of no more than might ordinarily meet together for all duties of worship in one individual congregation. I have often heard it said, but never could yet hear or see it proved, but I have seen good proof of the contrary. However sure I am, if union in a particular congregation is good, union in the Churches of two or three nations is better; for *Bonum quo communius co melius*. And I am sure the reasons on which the Apostle urges this care of unity on the Ephesians, binds not only to a particular congregation, but to all on whom the Name of Christ is called. There is one body, one Spirit, one hope of calling, one Lord, one faith, one baptism, one God and Father of all; not only the saints on earth. And Christ gave Apostles, Prophets, *etc.* for the work of the ministry, for the perfecting of the saints, for the edifying of the body of Christ (not till those of this or that congregation come, but until we all come in the unity of the faith). And I am sure the prayer which our Lord Jesus Christ made was not only for a, "particular congregation," but, "for all that should believe in him, that they all might be one," and that not by a spiritual and mystical union only, but by a visible union, such a union as the world might take notice of, "That they may be one in us, that the world may believe that thou hast sent me," (verse 21), "That they may be perfect in one, that the world may know that thou hast sent me," (verse 15). And I am sure the time will come when all that believe in Christ shall be visibly one, when the Lord Jesus having, "destroyed the antichrist" and all his other enemies, "there shall be one sheepfold, and one Shepherd," (John 10:16). And therefore I think we ought to desire, not only that all the Churches in the three kingdoms, but that all the Churches in the world may be one in doctrine, discipline, worship, and government according to the Word of God. And to endeavor it as much as in us lies.

Use 2. This truth, that it is the duty of all those that would walk worthy of the Gospel, to endeavor a sweet, close, holy, lasting union among themselves, calls us to bewail the great lack of that unity that should be among God's people, and such as profess to desire to walk worthy of the Gospel, and not only want of unity but want of care and endeavor after that unity, which is *too* discernible in these times in which we live. We live (beloved) in very sad times, sometimes

I am even ready to call them (in respect of the breaches and divisions that are among us) the saddest times that ever the Church was under. But I correct myself, when I remember how the Church of God in all ages has been exercised more or less in this kind with breaches and divisions. In the first (which were the purest, and therefore we may conceive were the most peaceable) times of the Church; in that famous Church of Antioch, where the disciples were first called Christians, (Acts 11:26), where they had the presence and labors of many prophets and teachers, as Barnabas, Simeon, Lucius, Manaen, and Paul, (Acts 13:1-2), yet even there, there was, "no small dissension and disputation," that within 4 or 5 years after the Gospel first came among them, (Acts 15:1-2). So in the Church of Corinth, within almost as few years after its plantation, there were both, "schisms and heresies," (1 Corinthians 11:18-19). In the Church of Rome, there were, "sects, or divisions, offenses," (Romans 16:18). Yes, and these dissension, divisions and offenses, were not only *inter plebem*, among the ordinary sort of Christians, but among those that were the pillars of the Church, the very Apostles themselves. So Paul and Barnabas, (Acts 13), in the second verse, had no small dissension with the false teachers in the 39th verse of that chapter, you read there was a very sharp and bitter contention between themselves. So Paul and Peter, there was a public contest between them; Paul withstood him, "to his face, and before them all," (Galatians 2:11,14). So in after times, the difference between Polycrates the disciple of John, and Victor, bishop of Rome, though it were in *re nihili*, being but about Easter day, yet how they divided and distracted the Christian world, and engaged, yea even enraged the eastern and western Churches one against another, *adeo ses mutno excommnincarint & anathematizarint*, that they excommunicated and cursed one another. I might mention the difference that fell out in after ages, between Cyprian and Cornelius, Basil and Domacus, Chrysostom and Epiphanius, Cyril and Theodoret, Hierom and Augustine, Prosper and Cassianus, Luther and Zwingli, Luther and Calvin. But I mention these things only that you may see that the differences that are among ourselves, among the godly, among the ministers, are no new thing under the sun; *sic sutt abinitio*, it was so in the ages that were before us; and therefore there is no reason that any of us should be scandalized or offended at them, yet there is reason that we should all bewail and lament them.

What sober, gracious heart would not bleed to see how small a matter some men make of dissenting from all the Churches of Christ, and embracing opinions, not so much new and strange as heterodox, witnessed against and condemned by all the Churches? To see how many under pretense of pursuing truth and liberty, have clean forgotten that there is any such thing to be regarded as unity. Everything to them that is new, is in their apprehension truth, and everything which they think truth, they presume they have drunk in an opinion, to keep it to themselves according to the rule of the Apostle, it must forth, *Scire tuum nihil est nisi te scire hoc sciat alter.* To see how men multiply opinions, and roll and run from one error to another, waxing worse and worse, deceiving and being deceived, till at length they come to downright blasphemy, renouncing all ordinances, Scriptures; yea (we should tremble to think of it) some are fallen so far, as to renounce Christ and God himself; and which is worst of all (if some men's doctrines are true) all thus must and ought to be tolerated; and it is now (in some men's judgments) more lawful and safe for men to err and blaspheme, than either for ministers to reprove, or for magistrates to repress these errors. But these things I had rather mourn over, than speak of them. It is not words, but tears and prayers (if anything under heaven) that must heal these sad evils. To provoke you and myself to contribute something of this kind to this purpose, let me propound but two particulars to consideration.

First, consider the detriment and prejudice that religion suffers by the divisions that are amongst us. Secondly, consider the prejudice and detriment that we ourselves may suffer by it.

First, the divisions and dissensions that are amongst those that profess the Gospel, brings a great deal of scandal on religion itself, and on the Gospel which we profess. I dare confidently speak it, there is scarcely any one thing that has been more prejudicial to the Gospel, from its first going forth into the world, than the divisions and differences which have fallen among the professors of it. Clement of Alexandria (who lived about the year of Christ 200, and in whose time there were more than 20, arch-heretics or masters of opinions in the Church, who had every one of them their peculiar disciples, *&* *catus Ecclesiasticos*, and peculiar Church meetings, among whom, *doctissimi and excellentissimi viri reperiebantur*, were some most excellent and learned men,) he tells us that the Jews and heathens in his time were accustomed to upbraid Christians with this, "You, O Christians, cannot agree among yourselves, but have so many, and so differing sects among you, who though they all challenge to themselves the title of Christian, yet they do all extremely detest and curse, and condemn one another; wherefore your religion (they say) can neither be true, nor come from God, otherwise undoubtedly it would be one, certain and agreeing with itself." See what desperate arguments against our religion our divisions furnish our adversaries with.

Philippus Camerarus tells a story of one who has sometimes been a Christian, a schoolmaster, but afterwards turned Turk, and was sent as an Ambassador to Stephen, King of Poland. Is *libere dicere solitus suit*, who was accustomed to profess freely and openly, "That he was moved to renounce Christ, by the notorious jarrings, and enmities and discord of Christians differing in religion; and showed a writing, *Valde atrox and amarusentum*, a sharp and bitter writing, composed by a certain Polonian; the scope of which was to prove that Mahomet was better than Luther.[26] These books, he says, the witness of your discords and heresies, will I now carry into Thrace with me, and will show to those of my religion, the vanity of your faith by most certain and real arguments." God grant that none of the scurrile pamphlets of these times fall into such hands.

It has been one of the greatest objections of the papists against the reformed Churches, that the dissensions among themselves are evident signs of a heretical spirit; so Bellarmine, Stapleton, and Becane. Fitzsnonde, an Irish Jesuit, has written a *justum volumen*, about the differences of the divines of Britain among themselves, which he entitles *Britanomachia*. It is true, *Qui tulerit gracchos*? And *Cledius accusat*

---

[26] *Et hos inquit libros vestrarum discordiarum and heresium testes in Thraciam nunc asperto. Musulmanis meis fidei vestra unitatem certissimis rerum argumentis ostensuirat.*

Machos? We could recriminate with ease, and turn them to Flarius in his tractate, *De sectis dissensiombus contradictionibus and confusionibus doctrina and religionis scriptoriu and doctorum pontificiorum.* Or we could remit them to Pappus, who has enumerated 237 differences they have among them. Or tell them of a Divine of Britain, that to requite the Jesuit's *Britainmachia,* has reckoned up 300 differences among them at Rome; and this might stop their mouths, but can never justify nor excuse our divisions; If there is confusion and division in Babel, must it be so in Bethel too? God grant our divisions do not give advantage to some of that crew to write a second book, *De Britainmachia* against us.

But if religion should not suffer by our divisions abroad, yet it suffers enough among ourselves here at home. For certainly there is nothing that more exposes religion and the intended covenanted reformation to obloquie and scorn, nothing that more confirms and hardens people in their idolatry, superstition, malignity, profaneness, atheism, than the woeful divisions that are among the godly party, the party that all this while have cried up and called for reformation. *Cum enim sine intermissione sic altercantes vident,* for when men see the endless contentions of those, who all profess themselves to be for truth and for the glory of God, that these cannot agree, one says, "This is truth;" another says, "That is truth;"

one says, "This is the way of Christ;" another says, "No, it is the way of antichrist." Men of profane and carnal minds take occasion from here to call into question, not only the things that are thus questioned, but all other points of religion, and think that all that which we call religion and divine truth, is but a fancy and opinion. One man thinks thus, another thus; but there is nothing certain. This makes men of carnal and profane spirits think religion not only a fancy, but a frenzy, "If the Church, (the apostle says) comes together into one place, and all speak with tongues, and there come in the unlearned and the unbelievers, will they not say you are mad?" (1 Corinthians 14:23). What will they say then, when in the Church they shall hear several and contrary doctrines, what a door this opens to Epicureanism and Atheism! What fatal and destroying stumbling blocks does this lay before the face of sinners? And how many poor souls may by this be turned aside forever from seeking after God, his ways and truth, the Lord only knows. But O that this consideration might help us to bewail these differences, and might be a means to heal them. I have read of Basil and Eusebius, between whom there was a great contest, that when they heard how the Arians, the common enemies of Christ and of his truth and Church, began to make use of their differences to prejudice the truth, and they presently laid their controversy aside, and both joined against the common adversary. We cannot be ignorant of what advantage papists and malignant people make of our differences, that it is a principal weapon by which they fight against the cause and work of reformation, a principal engine, by which they have drawn in and engaged many of the judicious multitude against us. And shall we yet uphold and continue our differences? Shall we yet put weapons into our enemies hands, wherewith to fight (not only against us, but) against the Gospel and truth of Jesus Christ.

Secondly, consider how prejudicial these differences must necessarily be to the godly party amongst us, I mean the whole body of those that have adhered to the cause of God and of religion managed by parliament, for I can by no means permit that title of godly party to be impropriated, engrossed, monopolized, as some would have it. There are two things that (in my eye) seem to threaten the godly part in this kingdom; the one is the rage, the bloody rage of the antichristian faction against them; the other is, their emulations and contentions against one another; and to me the later ever was a great deal more dreadful than the former. The rage of the enemies against them is extrinsic and accidental, but their divisions are intrinsic and intestine; and men die more frequently from intrinsic causes, from diseases bred within, than from such things as are extrinsic and adventitious to them; more kingdoms and commonwealths have been ruined by civil and intestine wars, than invasions and conquests. And if God should be so good to us, as not to suffer our rents to be our ruins, yet I fear (it may at least deprive us, of seeing that which we profess we would all be so glad to see) the peace of Zion, the good of Jerusalem, the Reformation of the Church, the Lord Jesus on his throne, "*Quam stulti essent duo volentes videre solem,*" Augustine says, "What a folly were it in two men that did both desire to see the rising sun, if they should fall a quarreling among themselves, which part of the heavens the sun would rise in, and how it might be seen, and in this controversy fall out, falling out in fighting, fighting to put one another's eyes out, and so when the sun riseth neither of them can see it." I need make no application of this to us and our times.

But where is the fault you will say? It is true, there are divisions, sad divisions, danger-threatening divisions among us, but where is the fault? I know there are many that lay all the fault on those whom they call *Presbyterians*, and say it is their rigor, and their pride and ambition, their spirit of domination that is the cause of all these divisions, so say the antinomians, and so the separatists, and so the Anabaptists, and so the others say. Now the Lord judge between us and them, and let his people that hear judge this day.

Who are they that divide in judgment from the reformed Churches of Christ in the world, that have opinions and judgments differing from the opinions and judgments of all the reformed Churches? We or the Anabaptists? We or the separatists? We or the......? Possibly they will say they are of the same opinion with the reformed Churches in fundamentals as well as we, and their differences, are but in *Minutiortbus*. Now supposing this to be true (as it may be in some of them) why then do they transgress the Apostle's rule? Why do they not, if it is in matters of lesser moment in which they differ from us, keep their opinions private, and have their faith to themselves before God? Why do they on so small differences (if the differences are so small) withdraw from the communion with us and the rest of the Churches, and gather themselves into distinct and separate Churches; some of them not holding one body with us, others neither holding one body nor one baptism with us? Their agreeing with us and the reformed Churches in doctrines that are fundamental; their holding one head and one faith, does not excuse them from being guilty of breach of unity and downright schism, as long as they do not hold one body, one baptism. *Schisma* (Augustine says) *est eadem opinantem & codem ritu utentem solo congregationis delectari dissidio.* Schism is, when a man that professes the same faith and worship, is delighted only with the difference of an assembly or congregation. And again, *Schismaticos facit non diversa fides sed communionis disrupta societas.* It is not a differing faith, but breaking the fellowship of communion that makes men schismatic. And again, *Schisma est, Recens congregationis ex aliqua sententiarum diversitate dissension.* Schism is a new or late dissension or disagreement of a congregation, arising from some diversity of opinion. It is Beza's observation that the Corinthians agreed in the fundamentals of religion, and yet they had schisms among them, from where he takes occasion today.[27] Schism or division (he says) is this, when men are so addicted to some men, or to some outward rites, that though they agree in the chief points of religion, yet they are estranged in their minds and engage themselves into parties and factions. Now who are they that though they profess to agree with us in doctrine, have yet made a secession, withdrawn themselves, gathered Churches, engaged parties? Consider and give sentence.

Who are they that have most broken the band of love? There is great fear what the Presbyterians will do if once they get power into their hands; but in the meantime, what do others do? Who are they that brand their brethren with the title, "Proud, Time-servers, prelatic, tyrannical, antichristian?" And what is this less than persecution?

Who are they that have been farthest from condescending to their brethren for peace and union's sake?

[27] *est cum alij alijs hominibus sive externis rittibus its sunt addicti, ut quamvis alioquin inipsis religionis capitibus consentient, tamen animis sin tab alienate and factions quasdam ineant.*

Were it fit, I could say something of this, yes much. I could tell you much has been yielded, yea almost anything but that one thing that would lay a foundation of perpetual division and disunion in families, Church, kingdom? Who are they that profess an utter impossibility of reconciliation or union, and plead for nothing but toleration, and some for toleration in the utmost latitude, to papists, Jews, Turks, (the very artifice by which the Arminians in Holland sought to gain a party and strength unto themselves), resolve these questions, and they will resolve you who are most guilty of these divisions. But as Augustine said sometimes of the original, so I say of our divisions, *Non tam inquirendam.* It is time better spent, to inquire how we may come out of them, than who has brought us into them. It was a memorable speech of Calvin, who said he would willingly travel over all the seas and countries in the world, to put an end to the differences that were in the Reformed Churches. And I think there is never a gracious heart, but would be willing to suffer banishment, death, yes could almost with Paul, wish himself *anathema*, accursed, so he might put an end to these unhappy differences of our unhappy times. Towards which, give me leave to speak a few words to you in a third use.

Use 3. This truth, "That it is the duty of all those that would walk worthy of the Gospel, to endeavor a sweet, close, holy, lasting union." Serves in the third place to exhort and excite everyone to these endeavors; and it is impossible to propound this exhortation in more persuasive and prevailing language than that of our Apostle, "If there be therefore any consolation in Christ, if any comfort in love, if any fellowship of the Spirit, if any bowels and mercy, fulfill you my joy, that ye be like minded, having the same love, being of one accord, of one mind," (Philippians 2:1-2). And O that I were able so to repeat these words, that they might reach not only your ears, but your hearts, and not only yours, but the ears and hearts of all that have a seed of grace in them throughout this whole kingdom. It is said of John the Evangelist, who was the beloved disciple, and the Apostle of love, that as in his lifetime he often and much exhorted to love, saying, "Little children love one another." So when he died, he died breathing out the same exhortation, "Little children, love one another." I think I could even live and die with those words of Paul in my mouth, "If there be therefore any consolation in Christ, if any comfort in love, if any fellowship of the Spirit, if any bowels and mercy, fulfill you my joy, that ye be like minded, having the same love, being of one accord, of one mind."

For *motives*, I will use but two; and you have them both in one Scripture, Psalm 133, the whole Psalm is nothing else but a commendation of this grace and duty of which we have been speaking. I intend not to undertake the whole Psalm at this time, but only cast your eye on the first verse of it, and there you read two things of this unity first, it is good; secondly, it is pleasant; and it is admirably good and pleasant. Behold how good! How wonderfully good? How beyond expression good it is, for brethren to dwell together in unity. Some things are good but not pleasant, some things are pleasant but not good; but unity is both good and pleasant.

First, it is good, wonderful and good in many ways; good, first in reference to ourselves, as it is an evidence of our election and grace, received from Jesus Christ. This may at first seem strange. Many do not think that a harmonious spirit sweetly complying with the spirits of God's people, desiring to keep the unity of the Spirit in the bond of peace; to maintain close union and communion with the saints, is as a sign of election, and an evidence of grace. But Scripture makes it so, "Father keep through thy holy Name those whom thou hast given me, that they may be one," (John 17:11). So, "and the glory which thou hast given them, that they may be one," (verse 22). "If there be therefore any consolation in Christ, if any comfort in love, if any fellowship of the Spirit, if any bowels and mercy, fulfill you my joy, that ye be like minded, having the same love, being of one accord, of one mind," (Philippians 2). This oneness then is a grace *peculiar* to those that have the fellowship of the Spirit, that have received the grace of Christ, that are given to him by the Father. Not that there may be an external and visible union where there is none of this, and so there may be an external visible faith, repentance, holiness in those that are not elect, that have no grace and true, real faith and sanctification; a believing, holy frame of heart is an infallible sign of election. So is a sweet, loving, peaceable frame of heart, a heart naturally closing with the Church and people of God, tender of differing and parting from them, studying ways of love and union, "By this shall all men know that you are my disciples, if you have love one to another," (John 13:35).

Secondly, it is good, as in reference to ourselves, so in reference to our Lord Jesus Christ, (if anything that is in such poor creatures may be said to be good for Jesus Christ), this unity among Christians, among professors brings honor to Jesus Christ, "That the world may believe that thou hast sent me; that the world may know that thou hast sent me," (John 17:21, 23); as if there were no such efficacious means to convince the enemies of Christ, that he is indeed the Son of God, and came forth from him, as this union and agreement of those that profess him; whereas on the contrary, disunion and discord among them, as you have heard all already, opens the mouth of our adversaries to blaspheme Christ and our religion.

Thirdly, it is good for the Church. This union is a great strengthening to it, making it look *terrible* or *powerful* as an army with banners, (Song of Solomon 6:4). The strength and terror of the Macedonian Phalanx lay in stirpations and condensations, in their thick, firm, close standing. So in the Church as it is in the body natural, not only the beauty, but the safety, the strength, the life of the body consists in the union of parts. The luxation of a member, pains, deforms the body, but the dismembering destroys it. This is also the case in the mystical body, the Church. The Church is a ship; let the winds rise, and the waves swell and toss. As long as the planks, the sides of the ship hold, there may be some possibility of outriding the storm, and escaping the danger, but if the planks and pieces of the ship start and fly one from another, there is no way but present perishing. *Laxis laterum compagibus*.

Fourthly, it is good for those that are without, it may help to ingratiate religion and the truth of God unto them, and draw on their conversion, "There is nothing (Chrysostom says) so attractive as love. For signs and wonders wrought by you (he says) men may emulate you, but for this they will admire and love you, and loving you, will apprehend the truth, and walk in the way. And if presently the heathen (for of such a man he is speaking) does not turn into a believer, wonder not, be not troubled at it; but suffer him to praise you and love you, and in time he will in this way come to be a believer." Behold then how good this unity is! Good for yourselves, good for the Lord Christ, good for the Church, good for those that are without; therefore for their sakes, for the Church's sake, for Christ's sake, for your own sakes endeavor after this unity.

Secondly, this unity as it is good, so it is pleasant. Behold how good and pleasant it is! And it must necessarily be so, if heaven itself is pleasant, for there is perfect union and harmony. In heaven they all think and speak the same thing, there are no divisions in heaven. And I am confident there is none of you that can imagine but if we could attain to such a union and harmony here on earth, it would be a most sweet and pleasant thing. For first, by this we should be the better enabled to praise and glorify God, "Now the God of patience and consolation, grant you to be likeminded towards one another in Christ Jesus," (Romans 15:5). To what end? "That ye may be with one mind and one mouth glorify God, even the Father of our Lord Jesus Christ." The more union and harmony among us, the more melody in our praises, the more glory to our God.

Secondly, by this we shall converse together with more joy and gladness, "And they continuing daily with one accord in the temple, did eat their meat with gladness and singleness of heart," (Acts 2:4).

Thirdly, by all this the Gospel and ways of religion will be rendered more lovely and amiable in the eyes of others. See, "Praising God and having favor with all the people," (Acts 2:47). It was not so much their speaking with tongues, or working of miracles, as their union and accord among themselves, that procured them this favor with all the people. "If men (Chrysostom says) should do ten thousand signs or wonders, and be at variance among themselves, they would be ridiculous. Where on the other side, if they love one another perfectly, though they do no wonders; they will continue reverenced and unconquered. We admire Paul, he says, not for raising the dead, nor for cleansing the lepers, but because he said, "Who is weak, and I am not weak? Who is offended, and I burn not?" For if you add ten thousand miracles to this, you speaking of nothing comparable with it. Nothing among the saints so amiable in the eyes of others then as unity, behold how pleasant it is!"

Now if any shall say, how may this unity be attained? *Hic labor hoc opus.* To give direction to this would be the work (not only of another sermon) but of a large discourse. For the present be pleased to take these few, but sure directions.

First, labor to get all our hearts convinced, that it is our duty to endeavor union. Until this is done, our hearts will never set to endeavor it in earnest.

Secondly, see our differences, our disunions, our rents, divisions, to be our sin, our shame, and not our felicity or glory, that we have so many differing opinions and ways.

Thirdly, examine ourselves everyone how far we have had our hands in these rents and divisions, either as authors, abettors, or encouragers of them, and so far as guilt cleaves to any of us let us be humbled for it.

Fourthly, see the beauty and comeliness in union, look on it not only as a duty, but as a lovely duty, as a pleasant duty, and this will make us not only endeavor it, but endeavor it in love.

Fifthly, get the graces that are conducing to it, "Be of the same mind one towards another," there is the duty, "Mind not high things, but condescend to men of low estate. Be not wise in your own eyes; Recompense unto no man evil for evil," (Romans 12:18). Could we thus be and walk, how soon should we be at one among ourselves, "Endeavoring to keep the unity of the Spirit in the bond of peace," (Ephesians 4:2-3). There is the duty, "with all lowliness and meekness, with longsuffering, forbearing one another in love," there are the graces conducing to this union, "Be ye likeminded, having the same love, being of one accord, having the same mind.", "Let nothing be done through strife or vainglory, but in lowliness of mind, let each esteem others better than themselves. Look not every man on his own things, but every man also on the things of others. Let the same mind be in you that was in Christ Jesus," (Philippians 2:2-4). There are the means of attaining to this duty. O that God would write these Scriptures in our hearts, root out the corruptions here condemned, plant in us the graces here commended, how soon should we see an end of our differences, and all the people of God be of one heart and one soul.

Sixthly, pray *much* for union. There are other things that we are much in prayer for, we pray for purity and reformation, and we do well; we pray against persecution, that the saints may not be persecuted, but how few pray for union, that the saints may not be tossed to and fro with every wind of doctrine, that the saints may not be divided in judgment and affection, though I do not know any Church blessing we have more cause or more encouragement to pray for than this. This God has promised, (Jeremiah 32:39). In praying for this, we are sure we have Christ joining with us. That prayer of his (John 17) is eternally present with the Father, and of eternal efficacy to this purpose. O therefore pray, pray, it is that which God has promised, it is for that which Christ has prayed. Pray for union among brethren, for union in the Church of Christ. Now the God of all patience and consolation, grant you to be likeminded towards one another according to Christ Jesus; that you may with one mind and one mouth, glorify God, even the Father of our Lord Jesus.